AF333659

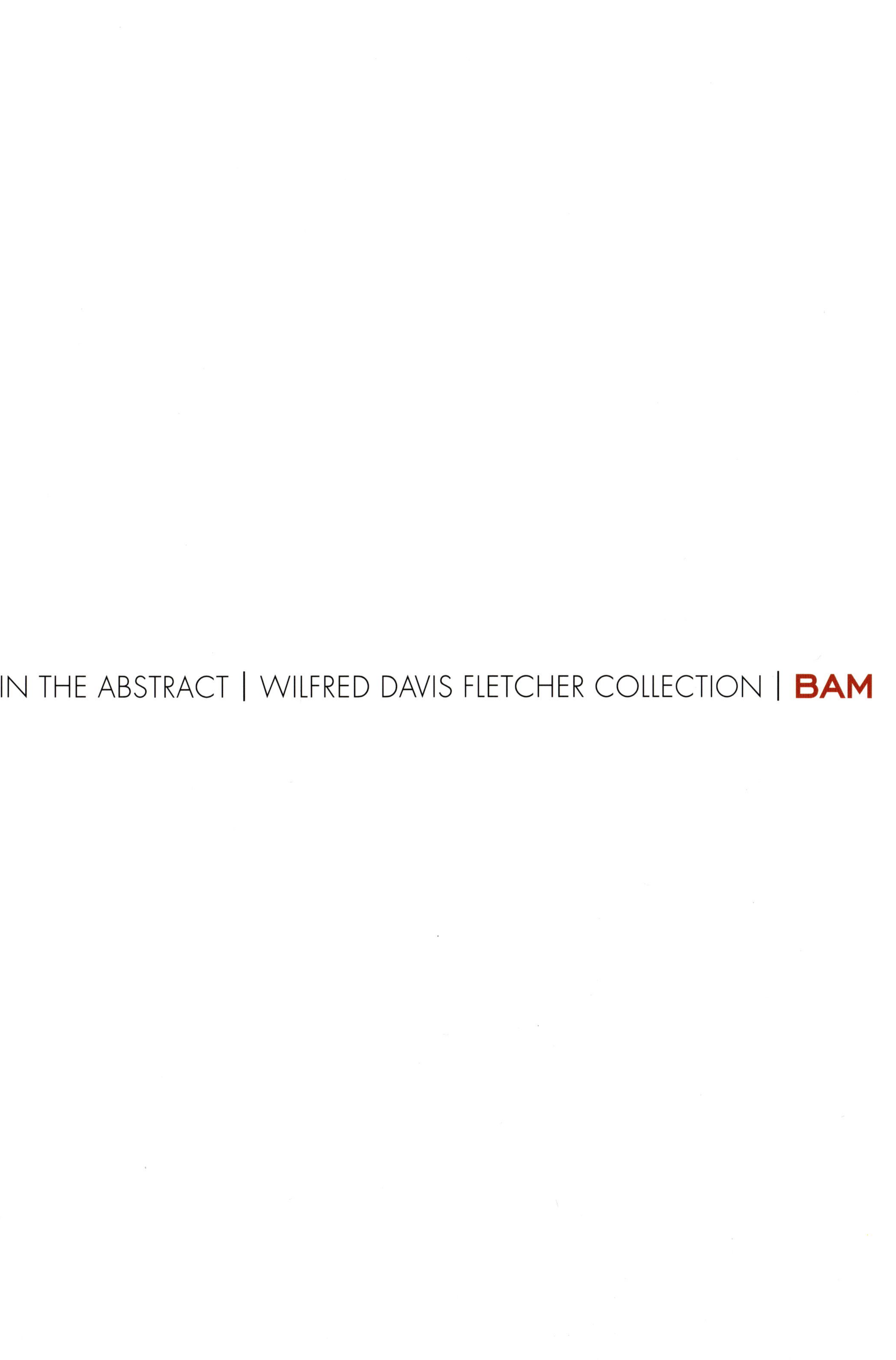

IN THE ABSTRACT | WILFRED DAVIS FLETCHER COLLECTION | **BAM**

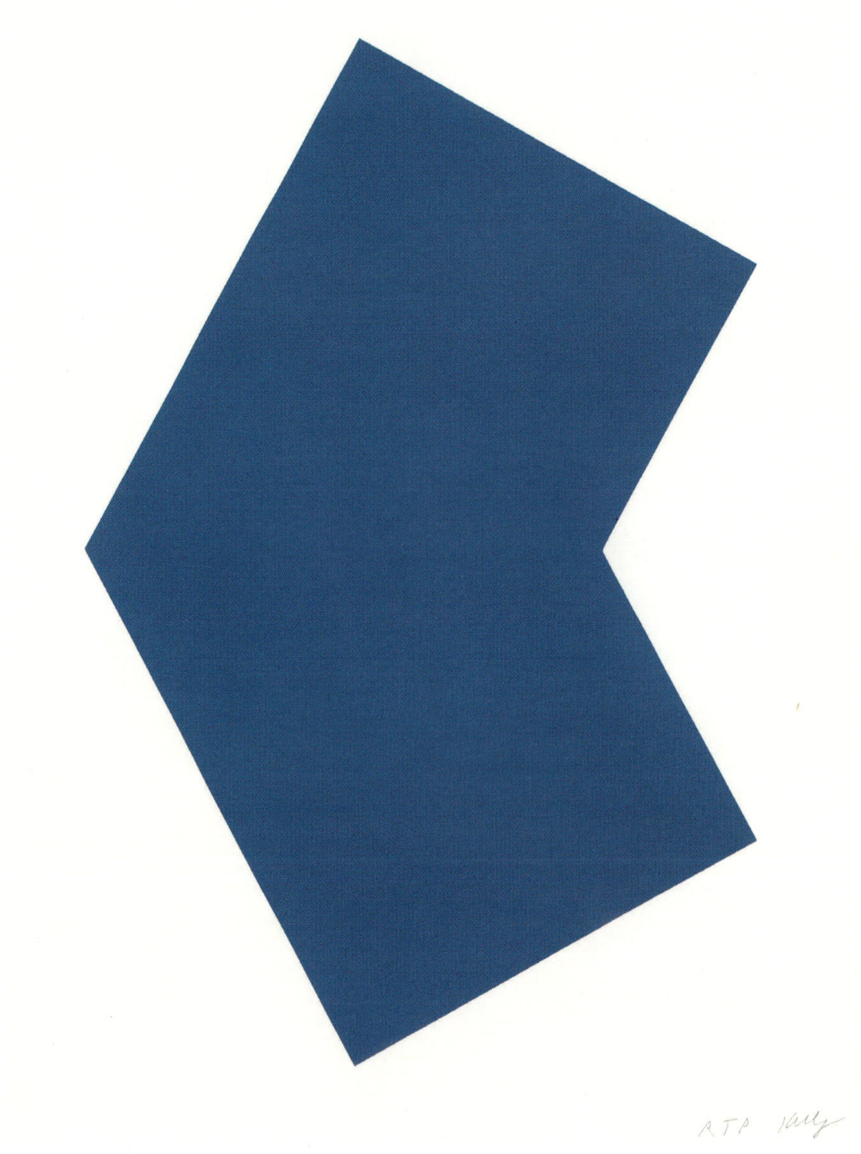

Ellsworth Kelly | Blue | 2001

IN THE ABSTRACT | WILFRED DAVIS FLETCHER COLLECTION | BOISE ART MUSEUM

PAINTINGS | SCULPTURE | PRINTS | CERAMICS | GLASS | WORKS ON PAPER

FOREWORD BY MELANIE FALES | INTRODUCTION BY SANDY HARTHORN | ESSAYS BY CHRISTOPHER SCHNOOR

CONTENTS |

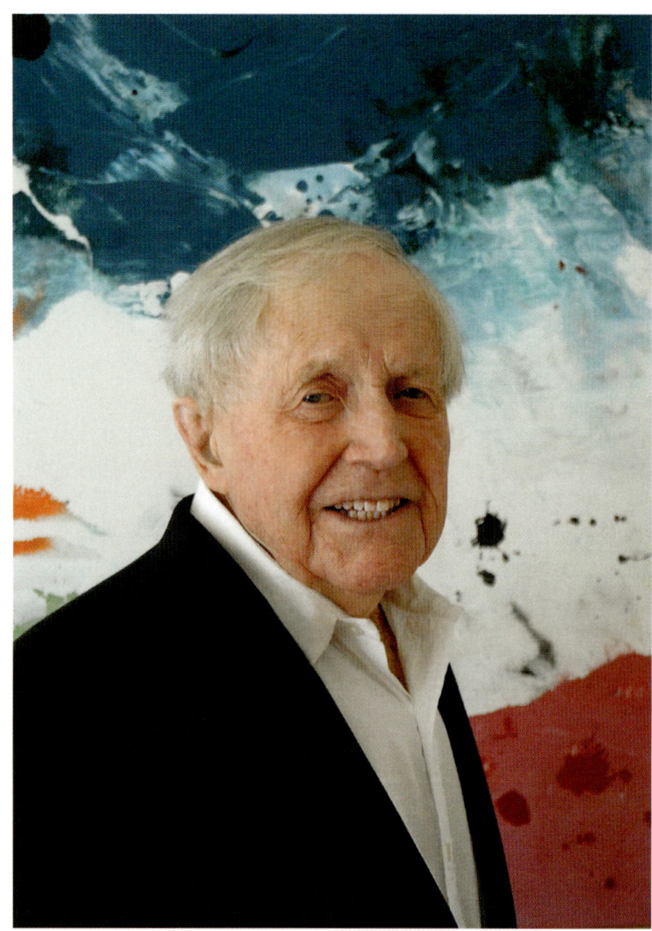

Wilfred Davis Fletcher

FOREWORD

Once in a while, someone of significance makes an unparalleled impact on an organization over his lifetime. Wilfred Davis Fletcher is one of those individuals.

Since his first gift of a graphite drawing by Maynard Dixon in 1984, Bill Fletcher has donated the majority of his considerable art collection to the Boise Art Museum. This publication celebrates his most recent gift of artworks, given on the occasion of BAM's 75th anniversary. The works of art hand-picked for presentation here are emblematic of Bill's vision and scope as a collector, as well as his generosity.

When the Boise Art Museum opened its doors in 1937, original works of art from private collections were shown, but the Museum did not yet possess its own collection. Seventy-five years later, through the foresight of a few and the contributions of many, BAM boasts an impressive Permanent Collection made up of 3,200 works of art. Bill Fletcher's gifts of art have both shaped and improved BAM's Permanent Collection. Over the past three decades, Bill has donated a remarkable 383 drawings, paintings, sculptures, photographs, prints, and illustrated books to BAM. Drawn primarily from his personal collection of 20th-century to present-day American artists, these gifts are an essential component of BAM's holdings of American contemporary art. His gifts also have included historical Asian and Native American objects that augment the Museum's collections in these important areas.

The Permanent Collection is at the heart of what we do at BAM, and we are fortunate to have a strong body of artwork from which to draw for exhibitions and educational programs. Bill Fletcher's gifts have been—and continue to be—an important part of our Permanent Collection exhibitions, greatly enriching the Museum's representation of the art of our time. This catalogue, along with its companion publication documenting Bill's 2002 gift of 120 artworks, provides a visual record of this lasting legacy.

For our 75th anniversary, the Board of Trustees of the Boise Art Museum established a goal of acquiring 75 additional works of art for the Permanent Collection. Bill Fletcher's gift alone made it possible for BAM to exceed this goal, and several other collectors and artists have followed in his footsteps by making gifts of art to the Museum in honor of BAM's 75th year. Collectors and philanthropists like Bill Fletcher are those who make it possible for museums to have a bright and enduring future.

The Boise Art Museum is proud to have collaborated with Wilfred Davis Fletcher in benefiting our community for generations to come.

Melanie Fales, Executive Director/CEO

Boise Art Museum is honored to celebrate Wilfred Davis Fletcher's extraordinary gift of more than 75 works of art in recognition of the Museum's 75th Anniversary year. For more than three decades, Mr. Fletcher has been a friend and staunch supporter of BAM. He is actively engaged with the Museum, visiting on his sojourns to Boise from his home in California and generously contributing paintings, prints, works on paper, sculpture, ceramics and glass, encompassing American art of the late 20th century, as well as a body of Asian and ethnographic art and cultural materials. This publication is a partial portrait of Fletcher's total collection and the companion volume to *American Art: The Wilfred Davis Fletcher Collection*, which commemorates his remarkable 2002 donation, comprised of 120 works, one of the largest and most significant gifts of art to come to the Museum since its inception in the 1930s.

Wilfred "Bill" Fletcher's magnanimous donations have altered the nature of the Museum's collection by introducing important artworks by prominent artists who were formerly unrepresented. Among internationally recognized artists whose works now enhance the collection are Jonathan Borofsky, Richard Diebenkorn, Mark di Suvero, Nancy Graves, Michael Heizer, David Hockney, Isamu Noguchi, and Richard Serra. Fletcher's substantial additions have also shifted the focus of BAM's collection by greatly increasing the range of abstraction and providing a more expansive perspective to its American art holdings. Since 2003, when the first major gift was presented in a comprehensive exhibition at BAM, works from the Fletcher Collection have been frequently displayed in Permanent Collection themed exhibits, enlivening and enriching the viewing experience.

Bill Fletcher, a third-generation Idahoan, grew up in the historic Warm Springs district in Boise's East End. He attended Boise High School and often visited the fledgling art center when it was first built in 1937 as a Works Progress Administration endeavor and then known as the Boise Gallery of Art. From childhood he was surrounded by artwork – his mother, Marie Davis Fletcher, collected Asian antiques and his grandmother was a plein-air painter of Idaho's scenic landscapes. Fletcher's delight in the arts was encouraged by his mother's enthusiasm and his family's ties to the burgeoning Boise Gallery of Art.

In time, the family relocated to California, where Fletcher attended Menlo College, followed by a year at Stanford University, a two-year stint in the United States Army Air Corps and later another year at Stanford. From there, Fletcher joined the family business, Fletcher Oil and Refining Company, in Los Angeles. Over the years, Bill Fletcher, always the outdoorsman, divided his time between Sun Valley, Idaho, and his residence in Palos Verdes Estates, California.

The artistic climate and access to contemporary art prevalent in Los Angeles and Sun Valley played a role in shaping Fletcher's ideas about collecting. Often visiting art galleries and learning from professionals in both locales, Fletcher developed an "eye" for art and zeal for the pursuit of intriguing artworks. He further established his unique aesthetic and deepened his appreciation for contemporary art by enrolling in studio art classes and visiting artists' studios and numerous museums. He started collecting in earnest in 1979, motivated by his enjoyment of the discovery process and the pleasure derived from living with art.

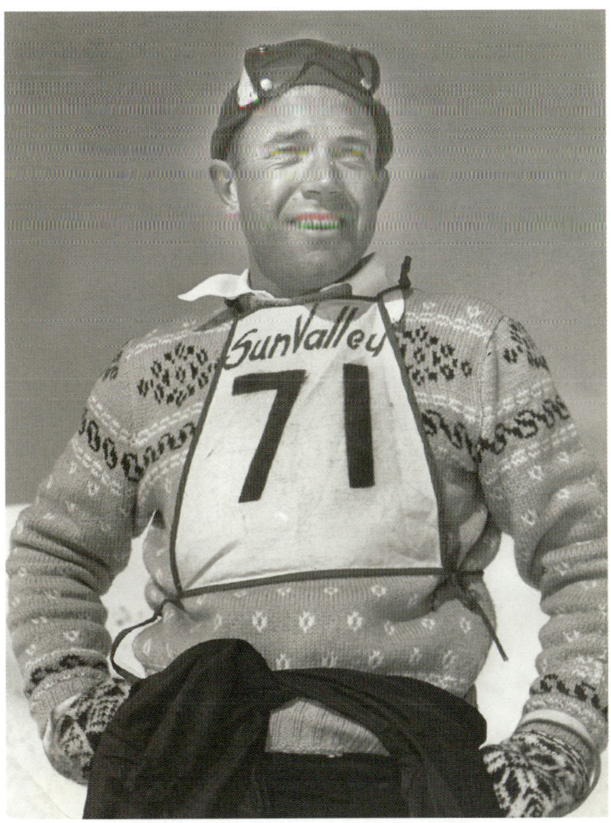
Wilfred Davis Fletcher | 1951 | Sun Valley, Idaho

Fletcher was particularly drawn to contemporary American art and began to assemble a collection generally reflecting four areas of interest: Los Angeles artists; artists associated with Los Angeles print workshop Gemini G.E.L. (Graphics Editions Limited); Northwest artists; and New York-based artists. These four areas illustrate the many facets of postmodernist aesthetics from the 1960s forward, expressed in painting and printmaking, as well as sculpture, glass, ceramics, and photography.

The Fletcher Collection highlights aspects of Los Angeles' artistic period of experimentation, multiplicity and flux that developed in the second half of the 20th century. Instead of a single defining aesthetic, numerous artistic practices offered a pluralist view. Contained in this volume are stylistic examples of California Pop art (Jim Dine); new realism (Michael Beck); lyrical abstraction (Charles Arnoldi, Sam Francis and Laddie John Dill); and the California ceramics movement (James Lovera, Peter Shire and Peter Voulkos).

An aspect of the Fletcher Collection owes a debt to the regional influence and importance of Gemini G.E.L., a commercial enterprise set up in 1966 in Los Angeles to publish fine art prints. Four artists from this 2012 gift come via Gemini G.E.L.: Richard Diebenkorn, David Hockney, Ellsworth Kelly and Richard Serra, augmenting important prints by Jonathan Borofsky, Jasper Johns, Roy Lichtenstein, Bruce Nauman, and Robert Rauschenberg already represented in Fletcher's previous donations.

The Fletcher Collection also includes artists from Northern California and the Pacific Northwest, where regional differences in geography, light, weather and the impact of the studio glass movement have helped to further define West Coast aesthetics; artists such as Sonja Blomdahl, Dale Chihuly, Raymond Saunders and William Wiley are individually distinctive. Other notables in the Fletcher Collection are more regionally aligned with the East Coast, particularly New York, and characterize Fletcher's continued focus on abstraction, embarked upon from a variety of paths and forms, including painterly abstraction and minimalism. Among renowned artists represented are Pat Steir, Terry Winters, Richard Serra, Helen Frankenthaler and Robert Motherwell.

In addition to post-modern and contemporary art, the Fletcher Collection contains a selection of American historical paintings and drawings, Native American art and Asian artifacts, many objects with a stylistic appeal that complements the contemporary artwork found in the overall Museum collection. Paintings by Maynard Dixon and Joseph McMeekin advance the understanding of art in the American West.

During the 1980s and 90s the Fletcher Collection grew at an accelerated pace, developed with discernment and in tremendous range and quality. Just as Fletcher acquired significant holdings of American paintings and works on paper, he continues to expand the collection, adding new works by exciting young artists. For Bill Fletcher, the joy of collecting is clearly matched by his joy of giving. Through his incredibly generous donations he pays tribute to the citizens of Boise and the State of Idaho. By transforming his personal passion to a public legacy, Bill Fletcher has infused the Museum with the energy of his dynamic vision.

Sandy Harthorn, Curator of Art

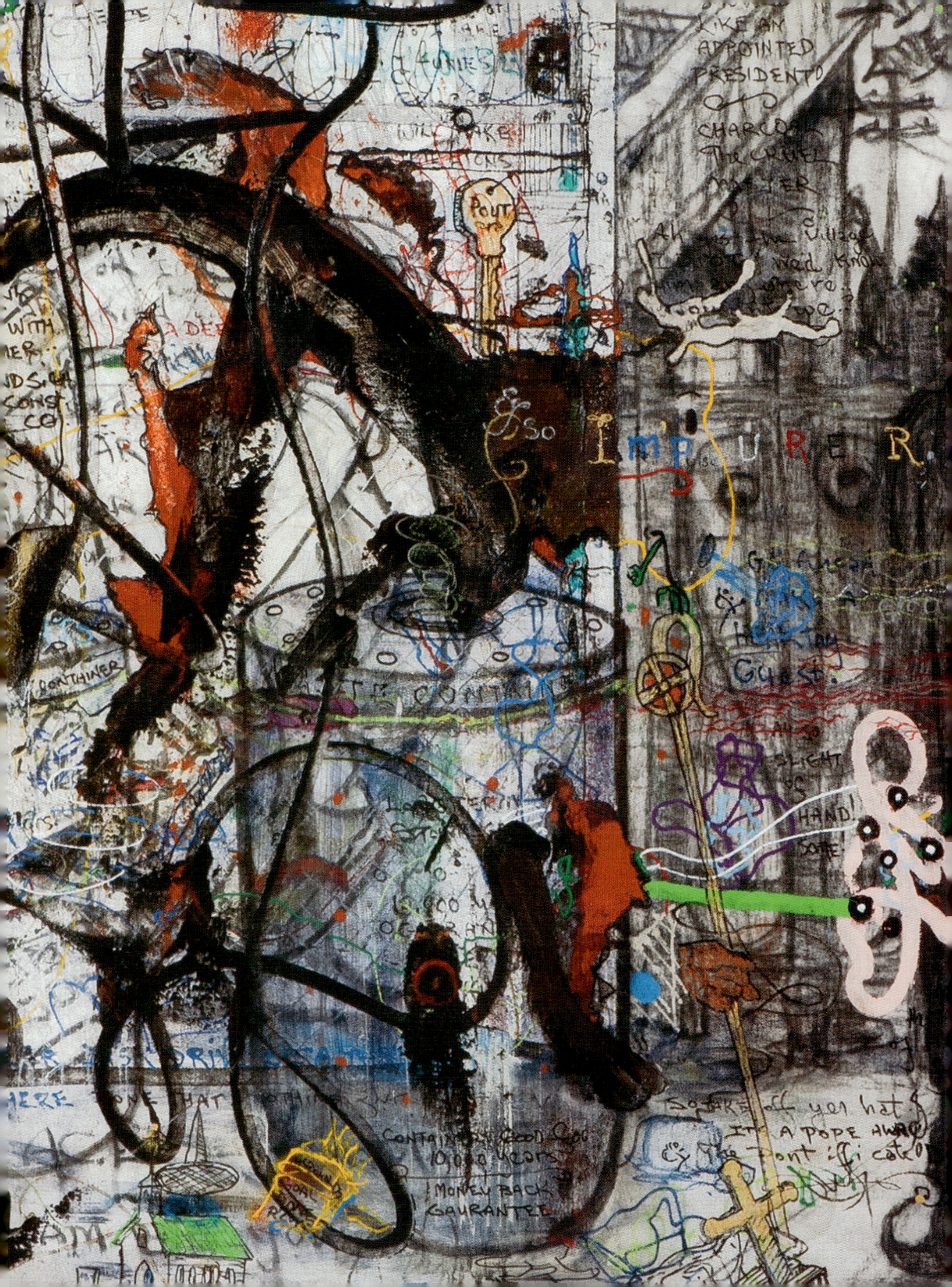

LIKE AN
APPOINTED
PRESIDENT
CHARCOAL
THE CRUEL
MASTER
POUT
E SO IMPURE R
GUEST.
SLIGHT OF HAND
CONTAINER
So take off yer hat
ITS A POPE AWARD
CONTAINER
MONEY BACK
GAURANTEE

P

PAINTINGS

As we saw in Wilfred Fletcher's first gift to the Boise Art Museum in 2002, this enthusiastic collector's taste in painting tends predominantly toward bold abstractions, compelling hues, and straightforward but strong compositions. Fletcher satisfies this personal predilection for such attributes of painting by surrounding himself with a mix of local, regional and nationally recognized artists, some of which are not known as painters at all, having instead a solid niche in other art forms. There is considerable overlap between the categories of art in this collection, which in itself leads to unexpected finds for the collector and viewer alike. Fletcher enjoys discovering the unfamiliar side of an artist whose work we thought we knew, often providing new insights into the artists of the period. This is particularly true in the paintings.

The works on canvas and the variety of other two-dimensional grounds he is drawn to the most reflect what has come to be called lyrical abstraction. A reaction to minimalism, Pop, and conceptual art that arose around 1970, lyrical abstraction incorporates a more intuitive, spontaneous technique characterized by free handling of paint, illusionistic space, and staining processes. As such, it is a descendent of abstract expressionism and color field painting. A number of the artists in this collection are associated with this loosely connected movement.

As the nature of his collection underscores, Fletcher is open-minded to the fact that a contemporary artist's oeuvre draws inspiration from more than one art form. To a large extent, this attitude can be attributed to the eclectic art scene of Los Angeles in the 1970s, 80s and 90s, which had a considerable influence on the direction of Fletcher's collection.

Take, for example, the paintings by Charles Arnoldi represented here. Arnoldi built his reputation as an unorthodox sculptor in Southern California, creating free-standing and wall-mounted sculpture constructed from rugged, found, natural materials that evolved into dynamic relief works with an unusual graphic quality and aggressive surface effects. This would become his signature style.

In Fletcher's second donation we are presented with a different Arnoldi, an abstract painter whose forms alternate between hard-edge and organic, and whose palette can range from the brash to the very subtle. Although his sculptural works have their painterly and drawing-like moments, they are a different breed of work. The eight-foot long acrylic-on-canvas *Volatile* (2005), composed of vividly colored rectangles, recalls the push-pull geometric abstractions of Hans Hofmann from the 1940s. It is more than that, though, as the artist skillfully incorporates hard-edge, Ellsworth Kelly-like forms with occasionally subtle transitions, smears, and a strategic use of black that evoke Mark Rothko's luminous, less insistent technique. Mondrian's formalism comes to mind, too.

In contrast, Arnoldi's stain-suffused acrylic on canvas from 1998, *Untitled*, is a soft-spoken, lyrical composition of floating ovals and irregular circles rendered in translucent blues and grays, dominated by a pair of black shapes in the lower foreground. The painting has the feel of a liquid, microscopic world in which tiny organisms bump into each other in a biological dance. Hardly a piece expected from a chainsaw-wielding sculptor.

A close colleague of Arnoldi's, Laddie John Dill, is a native of the Los Angeles area. The two met in 1968 at the Chouinard Art Institute in LA, later to become the famed California Institute of the Arts, of which so many West Coast artists in this collection are alumni. Their work also shares a number of characteristics, specifically a decidedly three-dimensional approach that crosses the line between painting and sculpture.

Fletcher has collected Dill's art in several media. Among them is Dill's 1982 *Untitled*, a case in point regarding the artist's marriage of elements from painting and sculpture. It is an example of the work Dill was perfecting in the 1980's, i.e., medium-to-large-scale wall-mounted constructions composed of cement, pigment, polymer resin, and plate glass on wood. The effect, as in much of his work, is of an enormous, landscape-inspired abstraction, with its forms suggesting continents, rivers and seas, and fields of glacial ice as if seen from space. Earth tones and thick, fractured surfaces evoke great mass and weight in geologic movement.

Raymond Saunders is another California-based, mixed-media painter with a sculptural bent, represented by two compositions (*Remembering and Then Forgetting* from 2001, and *Untitled*, 1995) which capture his technique of combining painting, drawing, and collage on wood grounds while remaining true to late-modern aesthetics. His, in a real sense, is a found-formalism which incorporates notations and references connoting broader social and cultural narratives based on the African-American experience, thereby setting him apart from such contemporaries as Robert Rauschenberg, Cy Twombly and Jim Dine. Nevertheless, all three of these artists have obviously been an inspiration to Saunders. Imposing, symbolic and enigmatic, the works are solidly abstract on one hand yet literary on the other.

An abstract painter in Fletcher's collection who established a working relationship with Frank Stella at Princeton University is Walter Darby Bannard, a 78-year-old artist from Connecticut with a solid reputation on both coasts. Bannard is an educator, writer and curator as well as an exhibiting artist whose paintings have been widely shown and collected by prestigious art institutions. His career has encompassed a number of different phases and styles, including minimalism (a Stella influence), color field, post-painterly abstraction and, of course, lyrical abstraction.

Bannard's large acrylic resin on canvas *Blue March* (1975) is representative of his shift in 1970 to using acrylic mediums, richly colored gels and polymers applied with a variety of non-art tools to create, as in this case, monochromatic yet agitated, scarred surfaces that provide a direct, sensory experience.

John Seery's artwork is probably the prime example of lyrical abstraction, a movement of which he was at the forefront in the 1970s, with *Art in America* calling him "probably the strongest…most exciting abstract painter of the moment." Seery was known for his sumptuous abstract oils that in scale and technique are not unlike Willem de Kooning's. However, the piece from 1973 entitled *Lenny* is acrylic on canvas, more a work of stain and splatter abstract expressionism than brushwork, and therefore typical of the so-called lyrical variety. The dark, densely-applied top of the composition hangs like an impending storm over a freer, vividly colored lower half, as if presaging the subject's sorry end.

On a smaller scale, but just as intense as Seery's paintings, is Daniel Mendel-Black's acrylic on plywood *Shifter III*, a bold yet loosely structured unframed abstraction that reflects the artist's aesthetic personality. Outspoken about his ideas on art today, Mendel-Black has written that he strives to "communicate the awkward grace of the living world," and he comes as close as he can while remaining committed to a non-objective vocabulary. With this piece, his overheated palette is kept in check by a swaying, sketchy framework that flirts with formalism while seemingly inspired by landscape. There is an undeniable brazenness to his work that obviously appeals to Fletcher.

Fletcher's attraction to vivid hues, generous application of paint, and idiosyncratic formal approaches is underscored in the work of other painters. Jonathan Lasker's expressionistic oil on canvasboard *Pictorial Regularity* presents dueling calligraphies of vivid impasto and broadly stroked black paint against a background of parallel black horizontal lines, creating a dynamically graphic visual vocabulary. Both intuitive and calculated, Lasker's formal choices compete but never clash, evidence that there is nothing improvisational about his work.

William Wiley, a founder of the West Coast Funk Art movement and a famous Bay Area provocateur, is a practitioner of numerous art forms. His oil on canvas *Canister Under the Banister* (2002) has a certain mania to it, typical of his oeuvre in general. A mix of cartoon imagery; metaphysical, geographic, political, and architectural references; and handwritten phrases, his work combines abstract expressionism, Bay Area figuration, and a satiric imagination. It is the summation of so much of what Fletcher finds fascinating in late- and postmodern West Coast art.

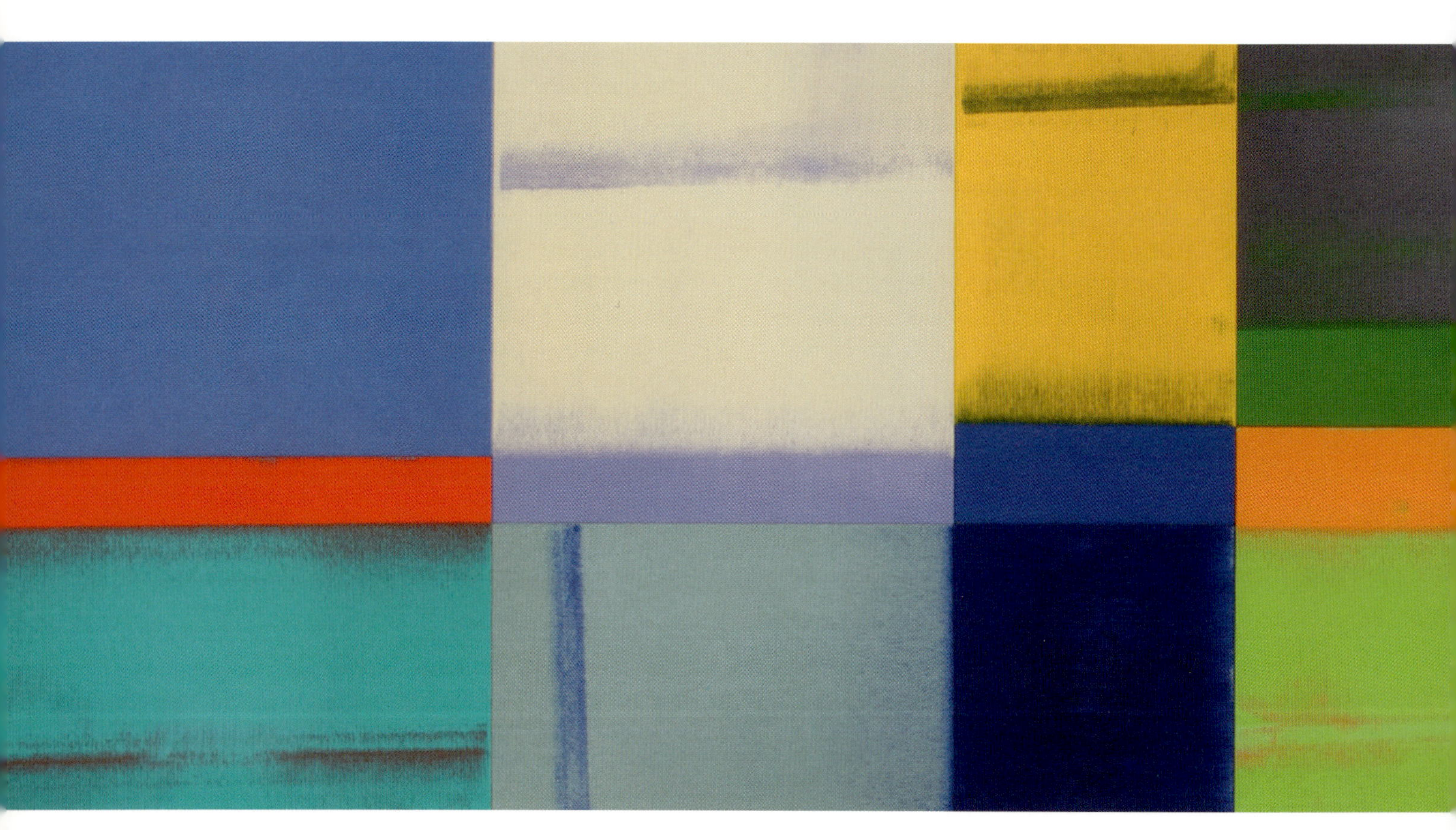

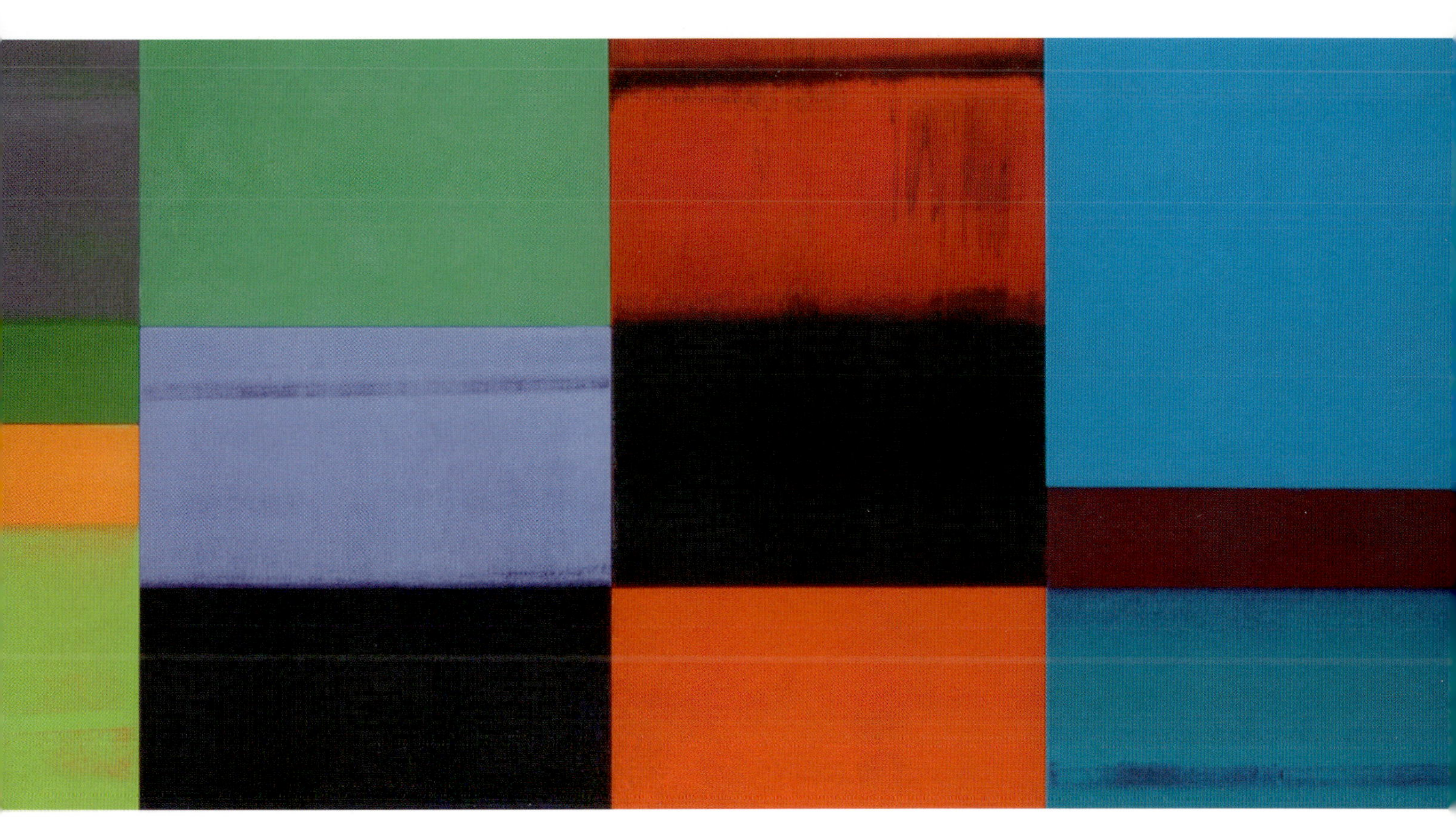

Charles Arnoldi | Volatile | 2005

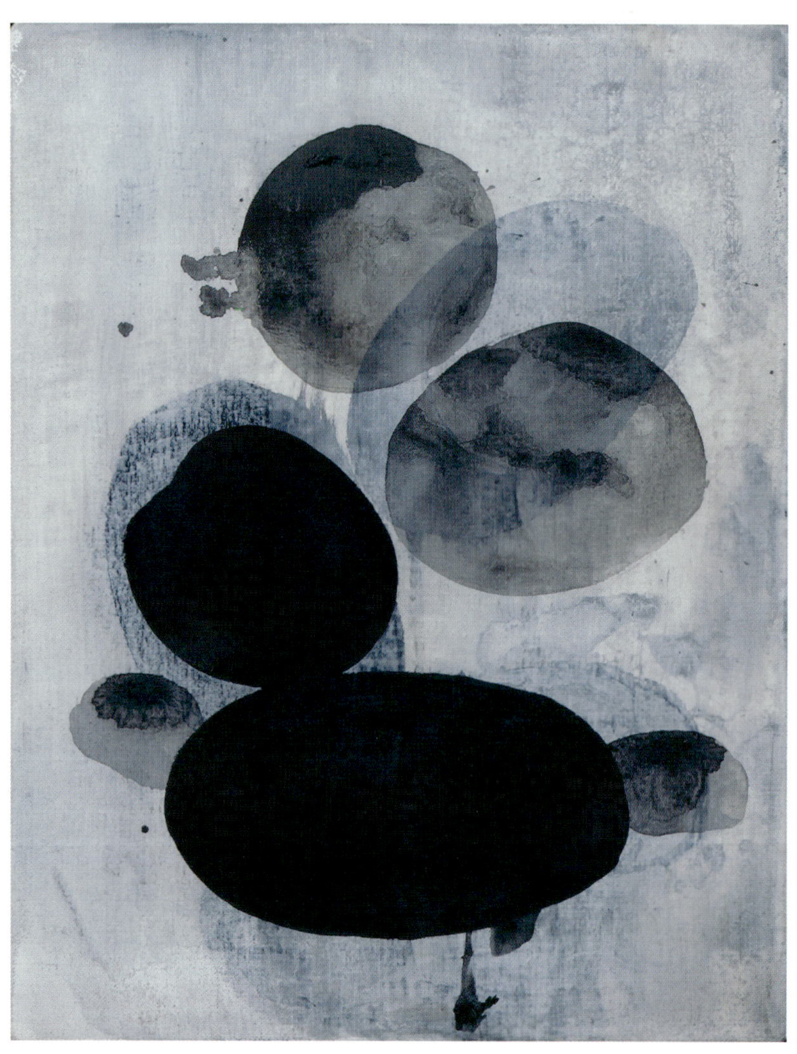

Charles Arnoldi | Untitled | 1998

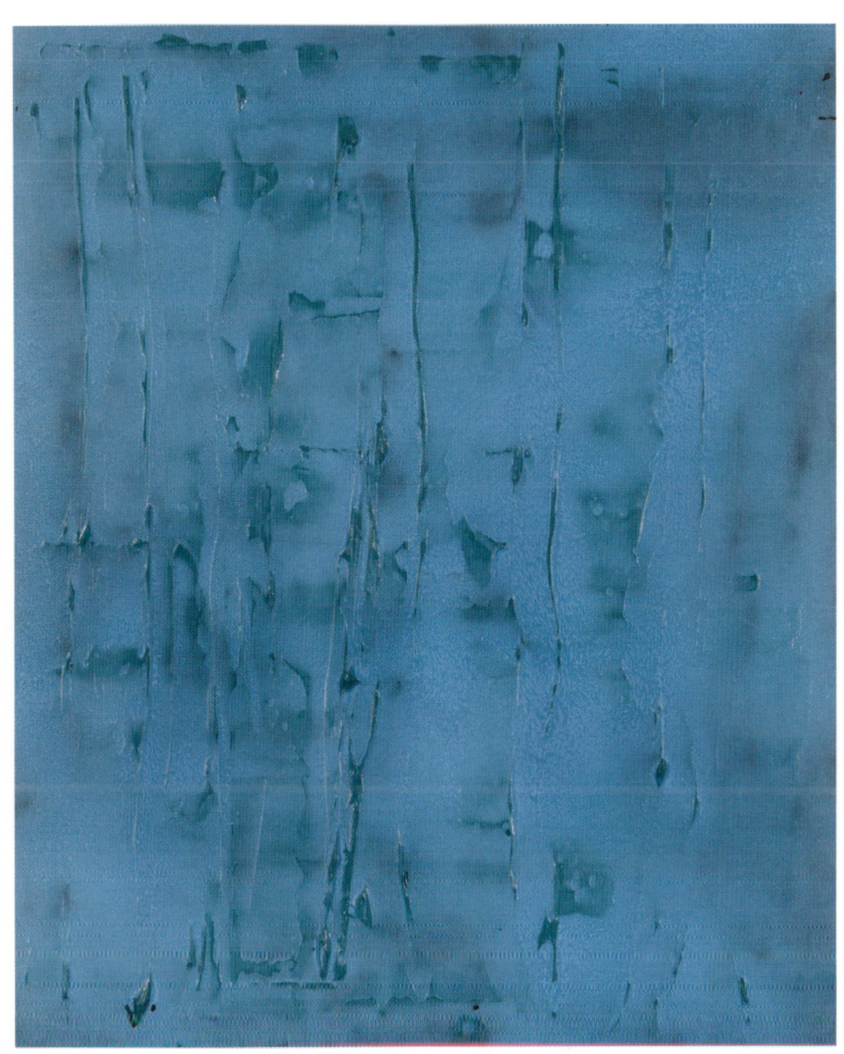

Walter Darby Bannard | Blue March | 1975

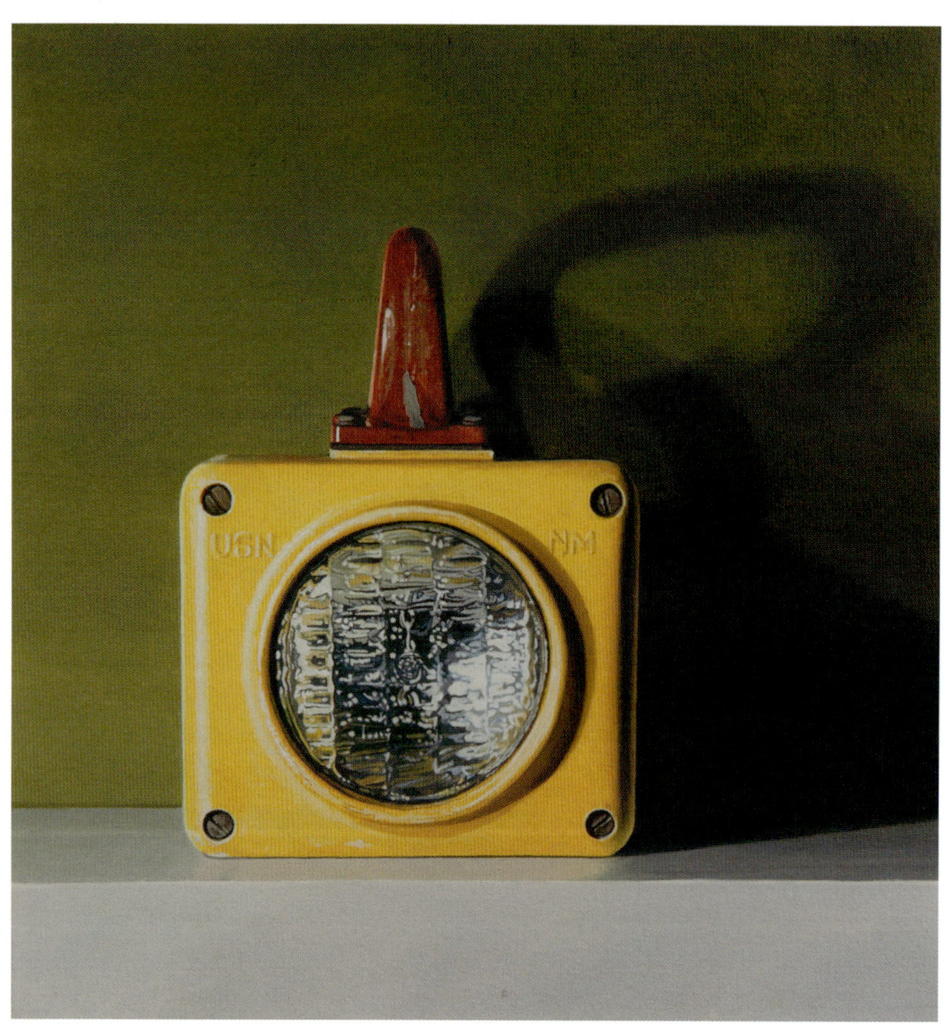

Michael Beck | Naval Maneuvers | 2006

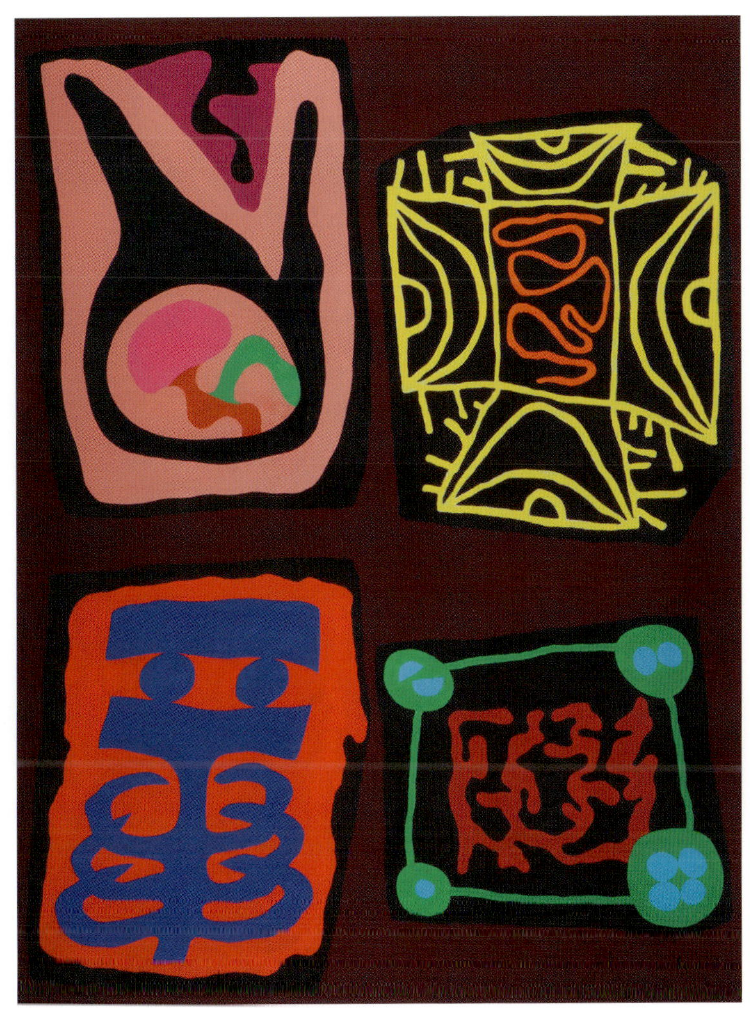

William Brice | Untitled | 2007

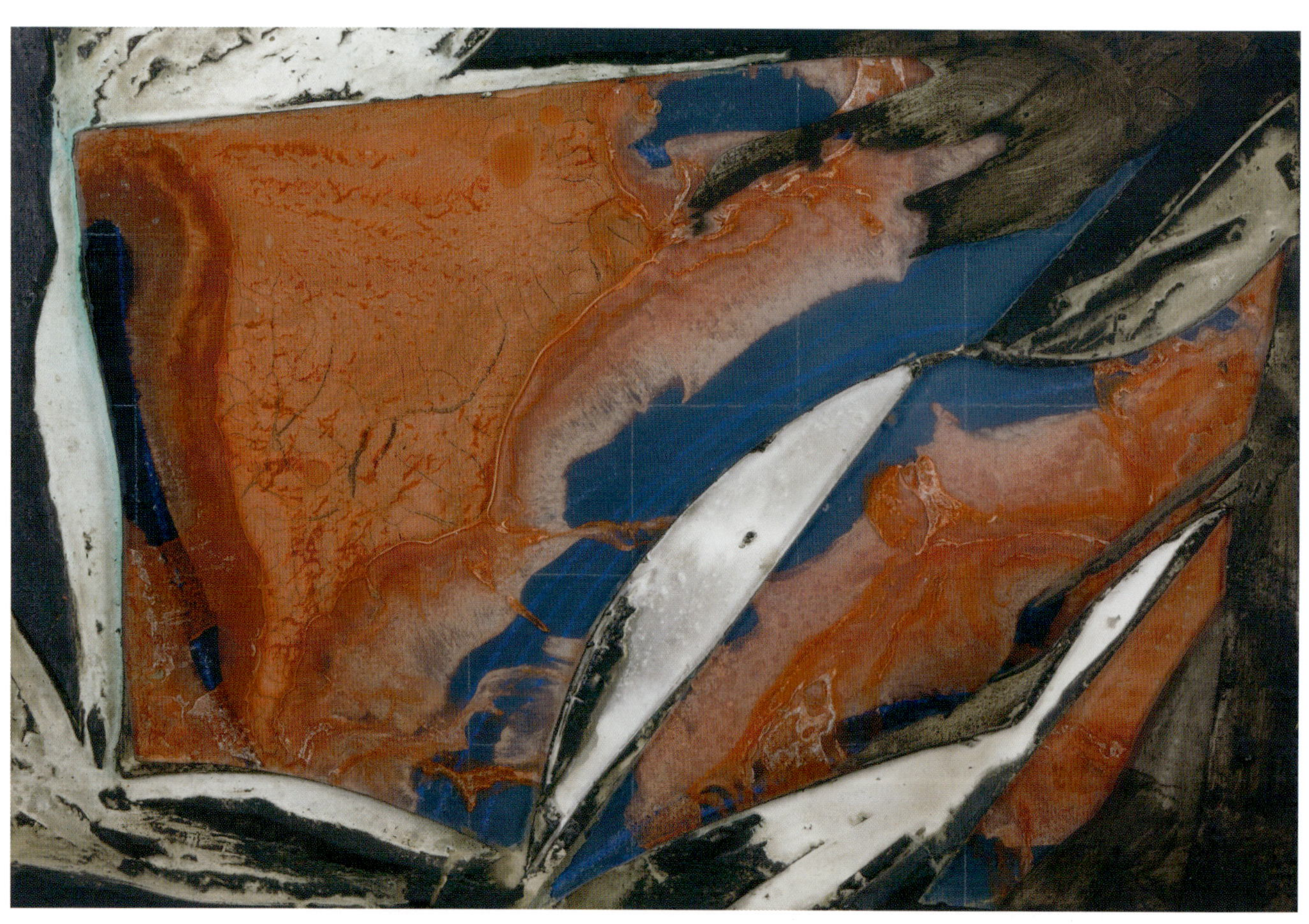

Laddie John Dill | Untitled | 1982

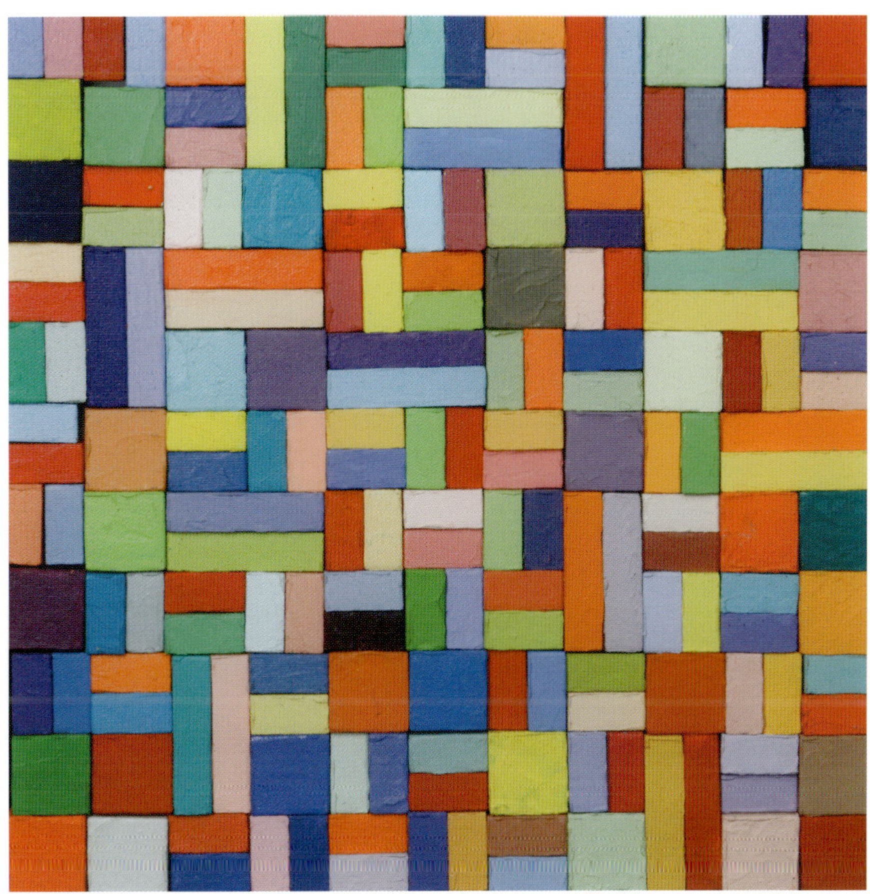

Carlos Estrada-Vega | Three Size Composition #5 | 2000

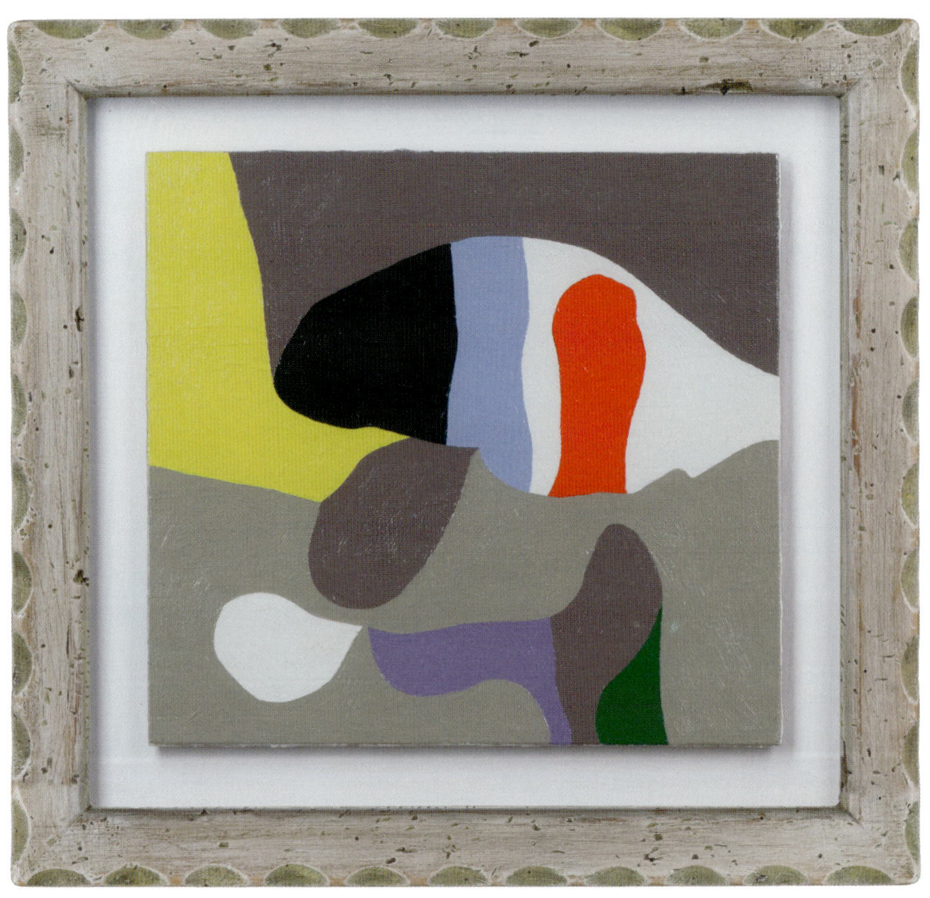

Frederick Hammersley | Ahead of time #2 | 1987

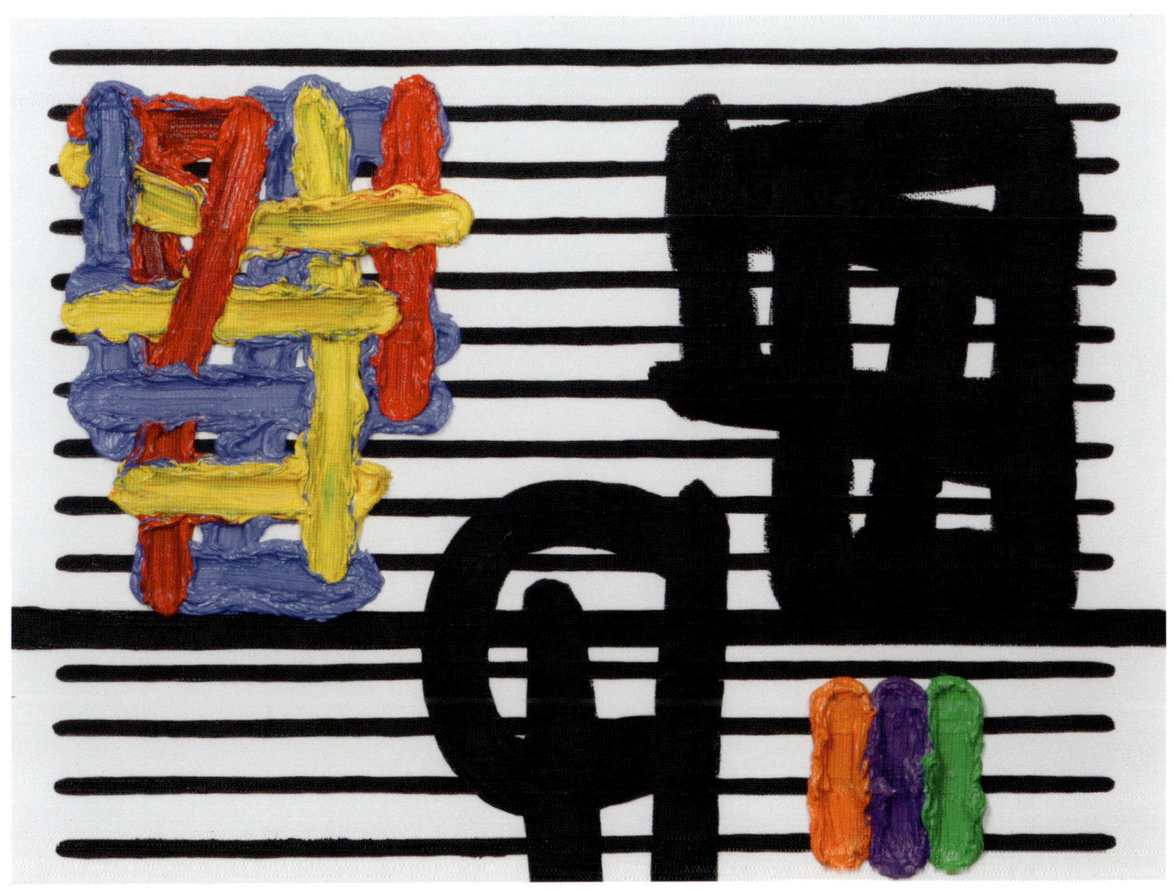

Jonathan Lasker | Pictorial Regularity | 2009

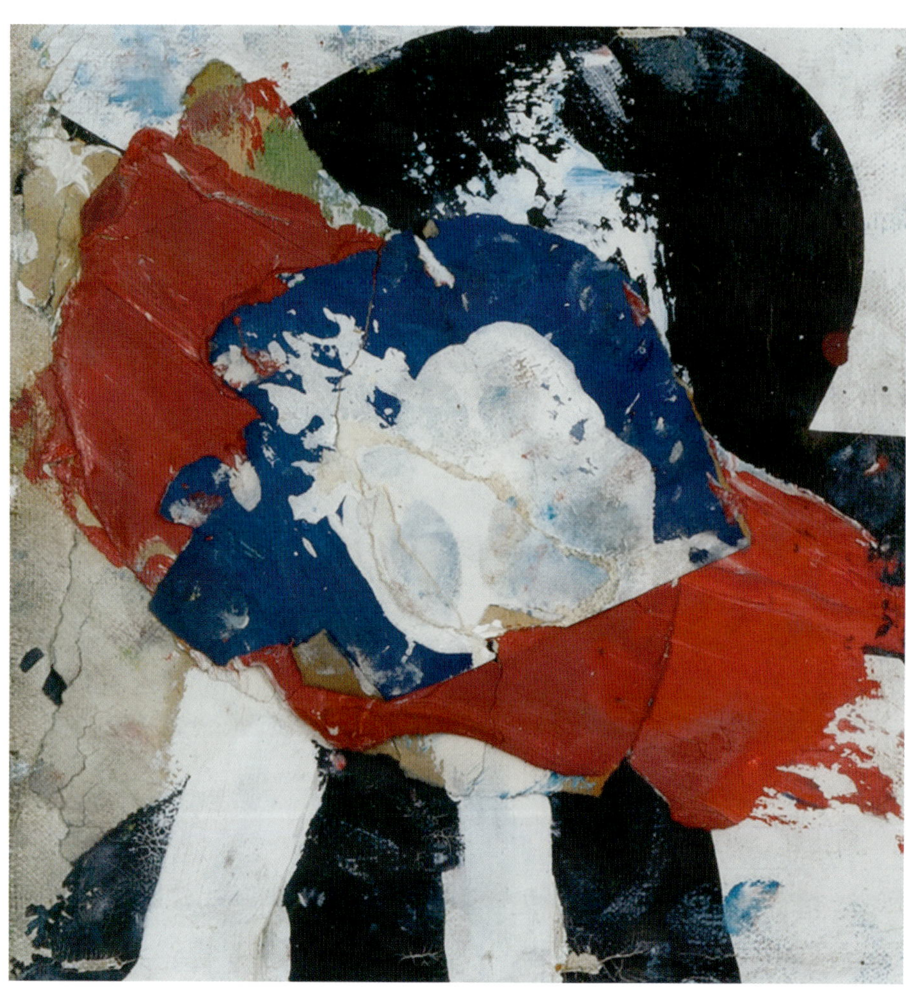

Alfred Leslie | Untitled | 1953-54

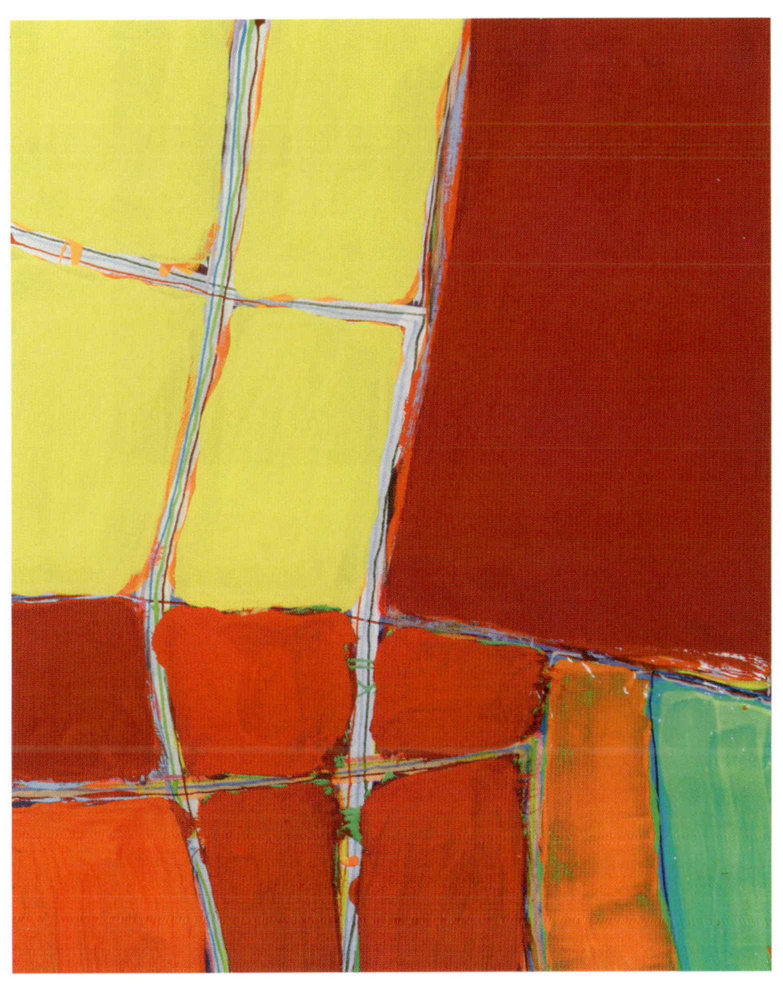

Daniel Mendel-Black | Shifter III | 2001

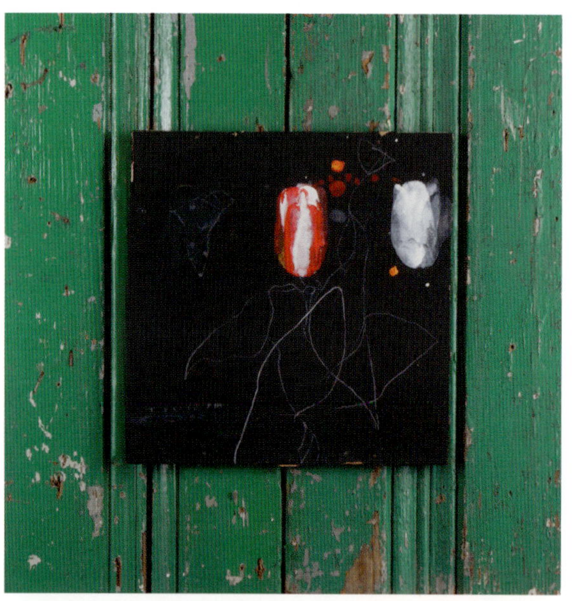

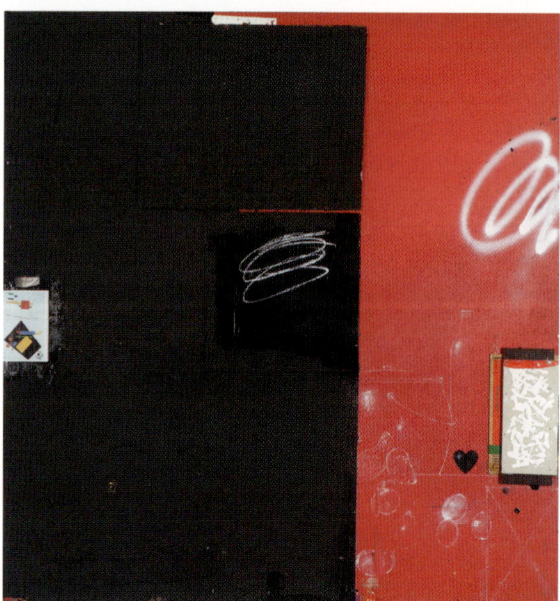

Raymond Saunders | Untitled | 1995 | Remembering and Then Forgetting | 2001

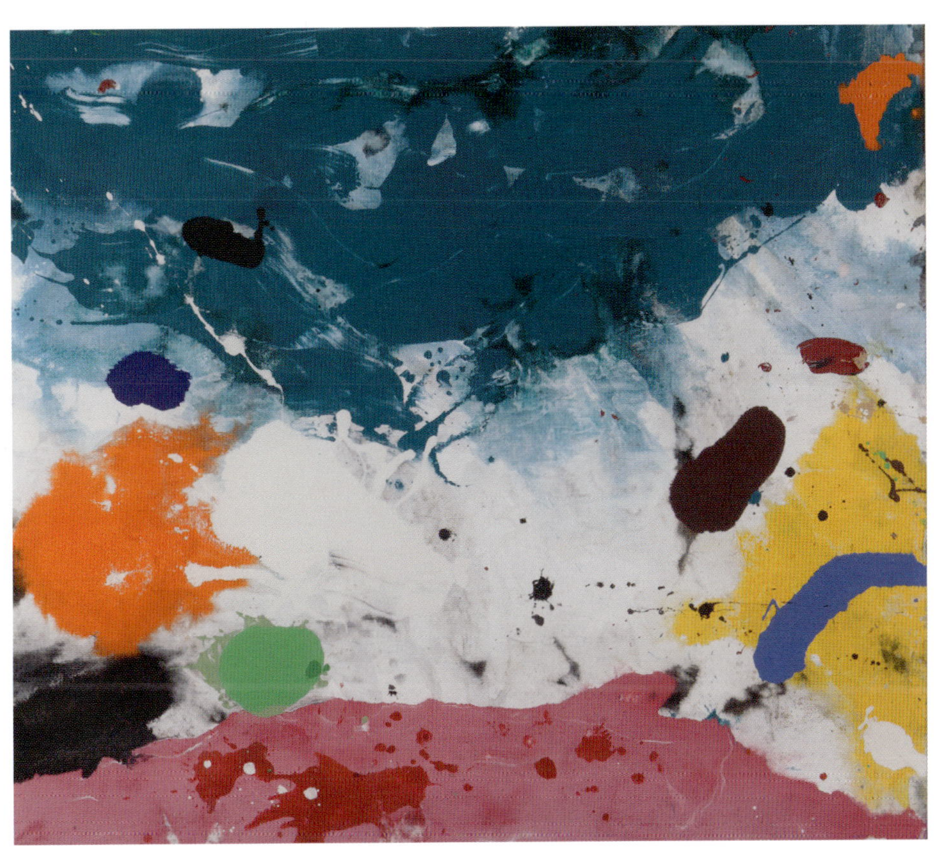

John Seery | Lenny | 1973

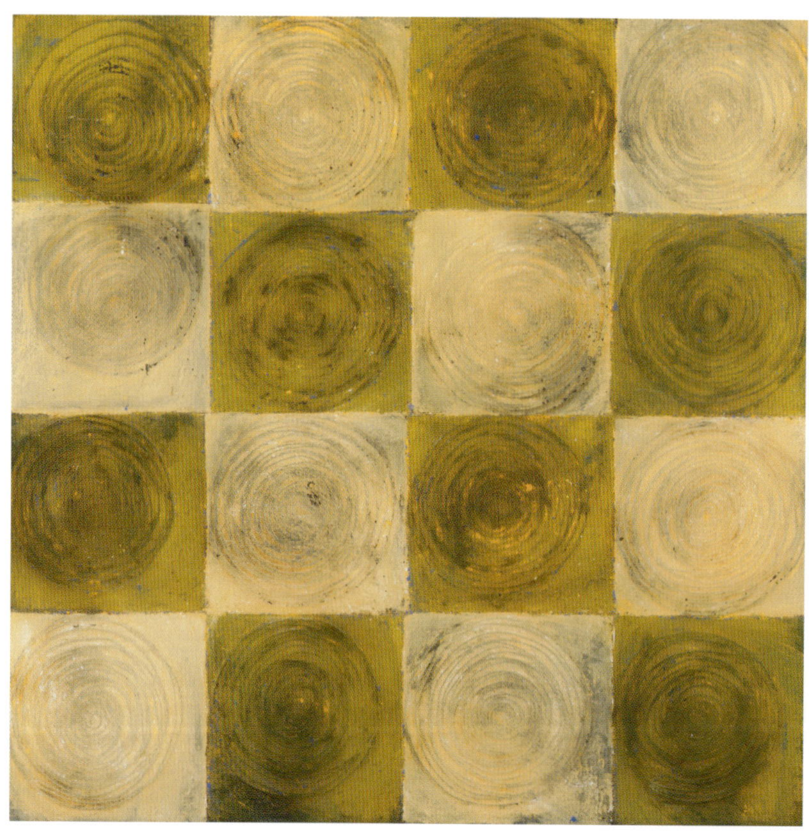

Sara Sosnowy | Small Circle Series 5 | 1996

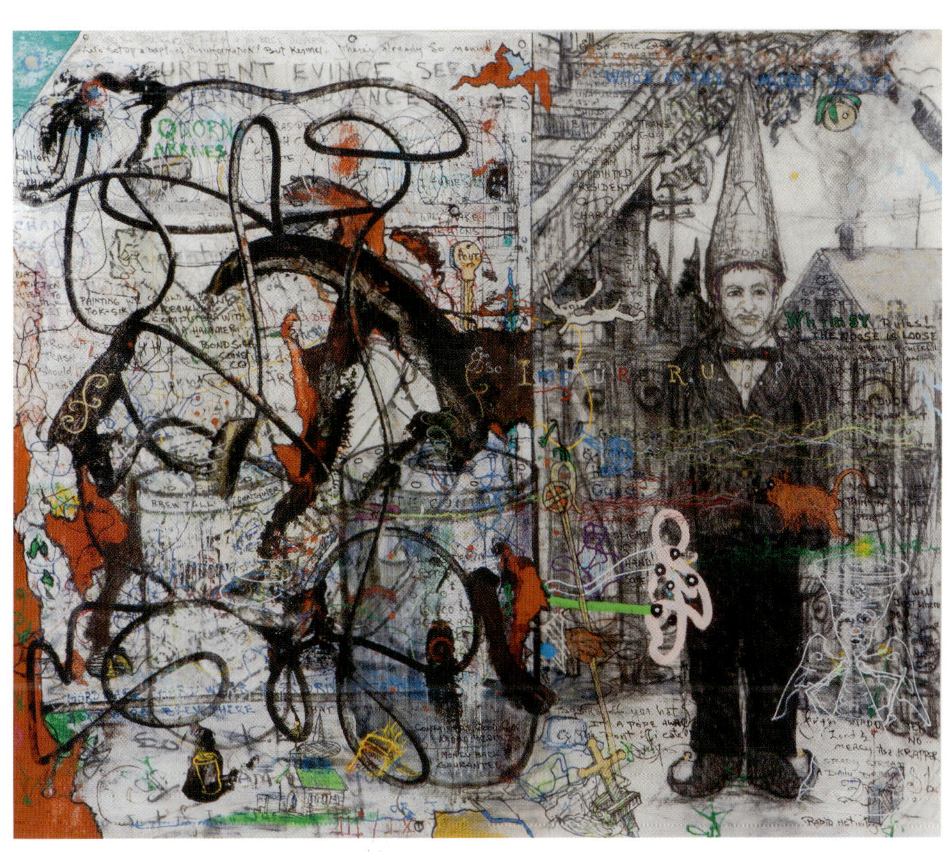

William T. Wiley | Canister Under the Banister | 2002

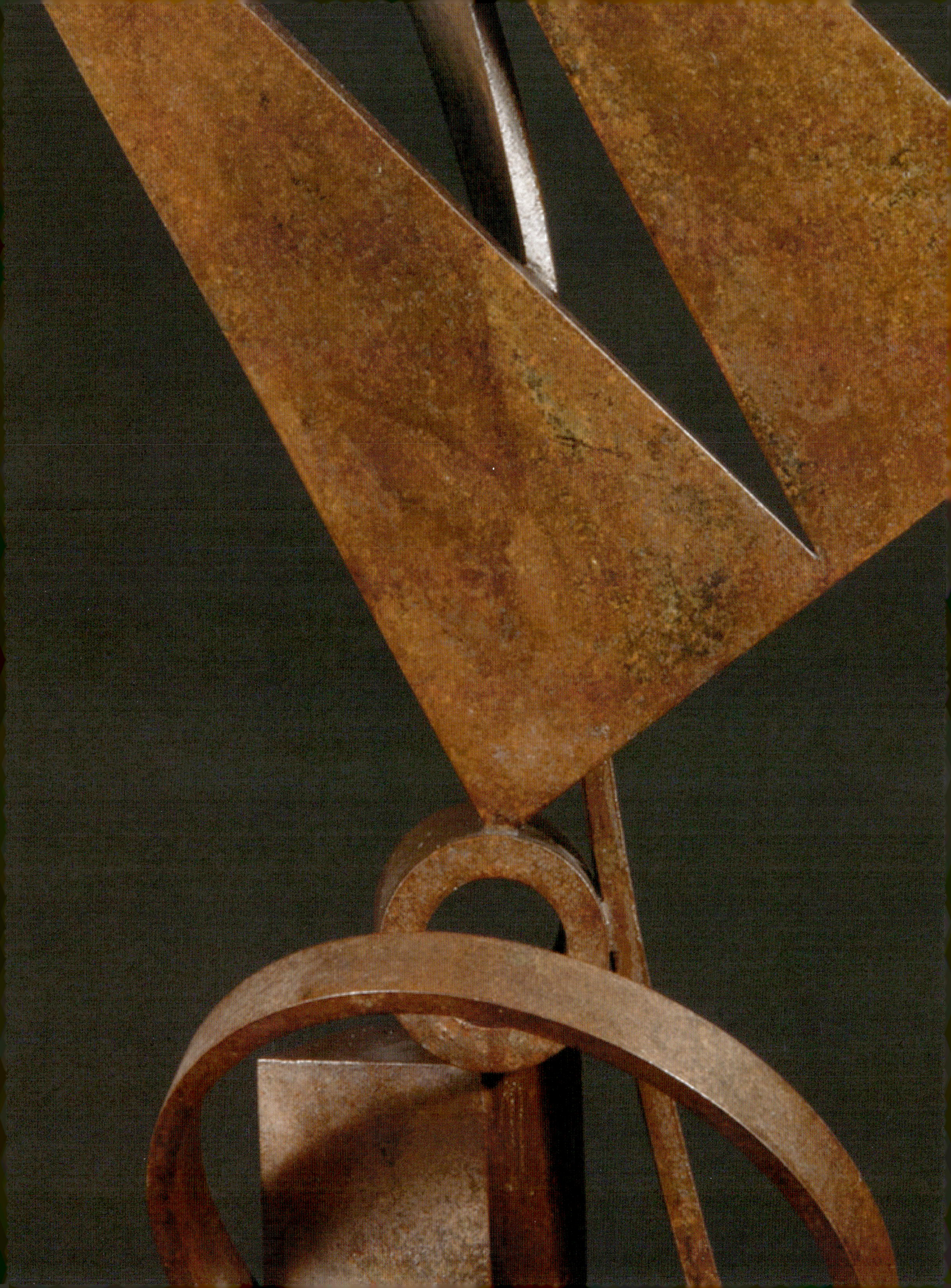

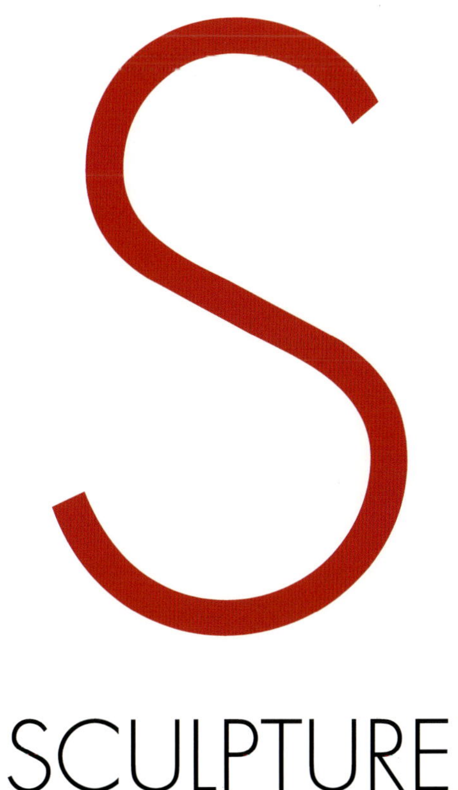

SCULPTURE

The sculpture component of Wilfred Fletcher's collection as represented in his gift to BAM shares several similarities with the paintings. Again, Fletcher is predominantly drawn, with some exceptions, to the aesthetics of abstract formalism, although on a less grand scale. Bold colors and graphic elements are still present, but these are not imposing, larger-than-life outdoor pieces. They have a more intimate element to them. Yet, as a fan of welded metal sculpture in particular, Fletcher has selected over the years a number of three-dimensional works whose forms have a monumentality despite their smaller scale. It is as if he strives to bring heroic formalism down to our level for viewers to better appreciate it.

Another aspect of abstract sculpture that appeals to Fletcher is the versatility of self-contained, unique intricate shapes that have a way of folding in on themselves or offering an array of perspectives within a limited sphere, as in the ceramics of John Mason or Peter Millett's work in metal. As with painting, the unconventional seems to capture Fletcher's imagination the most.

At the same time, Fletcher appreciates different approaches to the figure in sculpture. Several of the sculptors in this collection represent female subjects in non-traditional presentations, while others are figurative in the sense of referencing the human form, such as the bronze work of Bryan Hunt.

The work of Charles Arnoldi, in his more familiar sculptural mode, underscores the points raised above. *Untitled* is a mere 8" x 7" wall sculpture composed of panels of semi-circular, hard-edge aluminum painted red, white and blue in acrylic, thereby straddling the painting/sculptural divide. In reproduction, its broad planes of color seem massive, as if made of sheets of recycled industrial-strength steel, evoking the Constructivist project of the 1920s and 30s, an aesthetic echoed elsewhere in the collection. Its design and surface give it a presence way beyond its size.

The confluence of Constructivism, industrial form, and the occasional minimalist touch is evident in the work of several sculptors whose medium is welded metal. San Francisco artist Fletcher Benton first earned his reputation as a kinetic sculptor then switched to more traditional bronze and steel in the 1970s. One sees the impact of the great David Smith's late sculpture on Benton's constructivist architectonics and cubist insistence on the simultaneity of views. Benton's *Table 5* demonstrates an inventive dexterity with the acetylene torch much like Smith's. Fletcher has also collected the sculpture of Mark di Suvero, known for his enormous balancing acts of industrial and architectural metal forms, but represented here by the small titanium sculpture *Nukle*. This circular object with teeth like a mechanized gear evolves into a serpentine form that complicates its initial nuts-and-bolts demeanor, a different design concept by this artist.

In Fletcher's important donation, two other West Coast abstract metal sculptors are represented who, in their own distinct ways, combine industrial material, ideal form, and the interplay of inner and outer space. Guy Dill (brother of painter Laddie John Dill) makes welded and painted sculptures which show him to be a latter-day Brancusi preoccupied with essential form. His 1988 *Untitled Wall Sculpture* demonstrates how Dill likes to integrate ideal geometric shapes such as pyramids and cylinders in light compositions. The black patina he applies serves to emphasize these perfected forms.

Respected Seattle sculptor Peter Millett began his career as a painter, and in his turn to sculpture worked for many years in wood. His medium now is predominantly welded steel, with which he creates both freestanding and wall-mounted pieces. The larger *Octo* is a light-steel octagon created from triangular elements which set up a series of irregular rhythms, instilling a playfulness that Millett is fond of. He also encourages the viewer to circle the work as *Octo* will seem more substantive from one perspective, yet more empty and fragile from another. His cylindrical wall piece *Log* seems both self-enclosed yet open ended. Millett has a magician's touch.

The late sculptors Claire Falkenstein and Italo Scanga bring, via their presence, a broader art historical element to the collection. Falkenstein, who died in 1997, was a true avant-garde artist throughout her career, experimenting with materials as well as abstract form. She studied with the Russian Cubist Alexander Archipenko in the 1930s, was a close associate of Clyfford Still, who influenced her work, and lived in Paris for thirteen years (where she knew Jean Arp and Alberto Giacometti) before moving to Los Angeles in 1963. Her small-scale pieces in the Fletcher Collection are but a taste of the large metal-and-glass sculptures for which she became renowned.

The Italian-American Scanga (1932-2001) was an innovative sculptor who worked in a variety of mediums, often incorporating ordinary objects and materials, and who, despite his neo-Dadaist, neo-Expressionist proclivities, was strongly motivated by myths and the universal aspects of peasant life. His abstract wooden sculpture *Head 78* reveals the strong influence of Cubism in its competing planes and forms, creating a dynamic composition of simultaneous views. Furthermore, it is a three-dimensional painting, with a bold, abstract expressionist palette and technique imbued with strong graphic elements. Altogether, *Head 78* is a striking ensemble of momentous modernist moments.

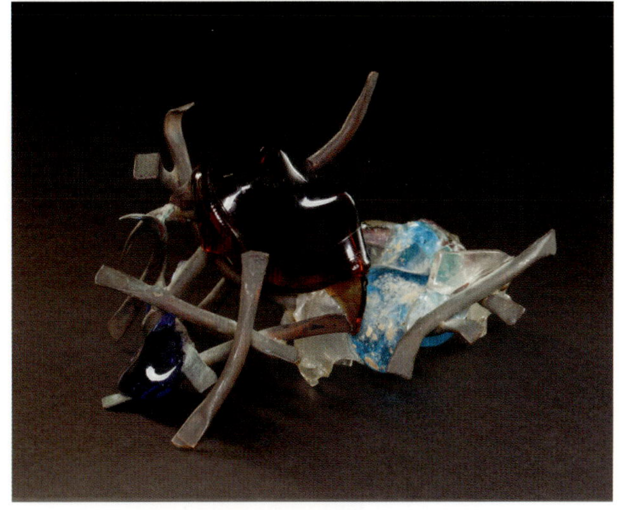

Claire Falkenstein | Untitled | 1959

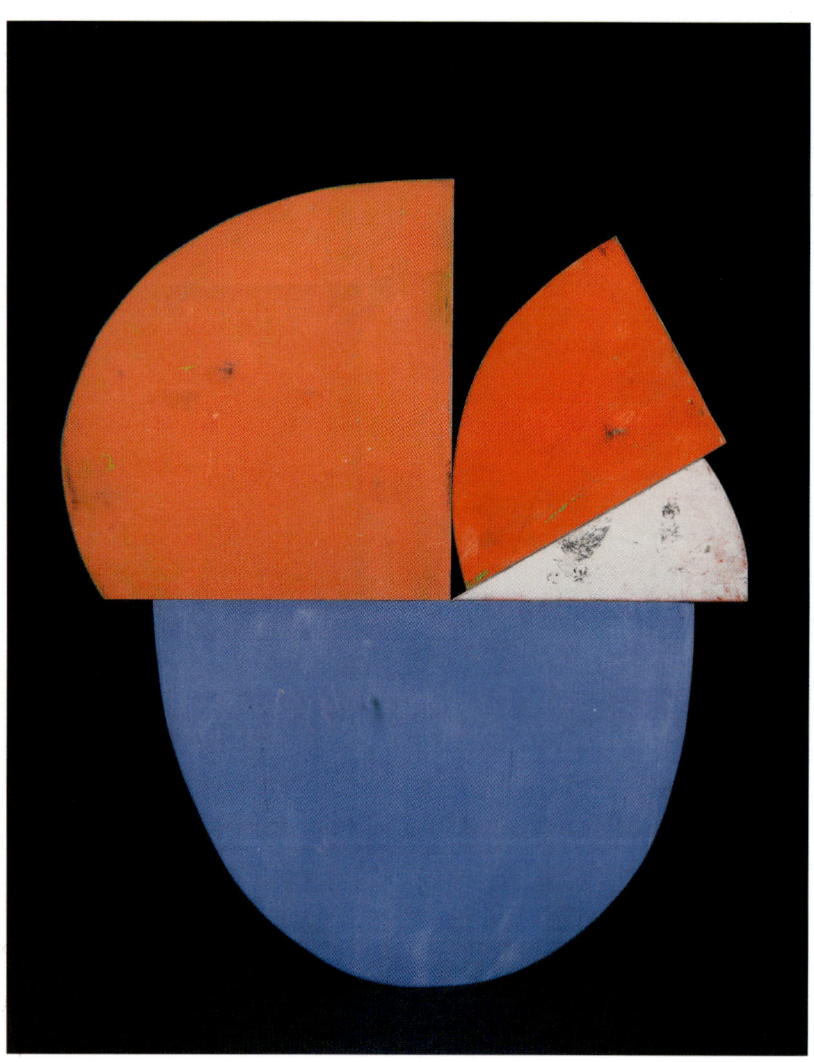

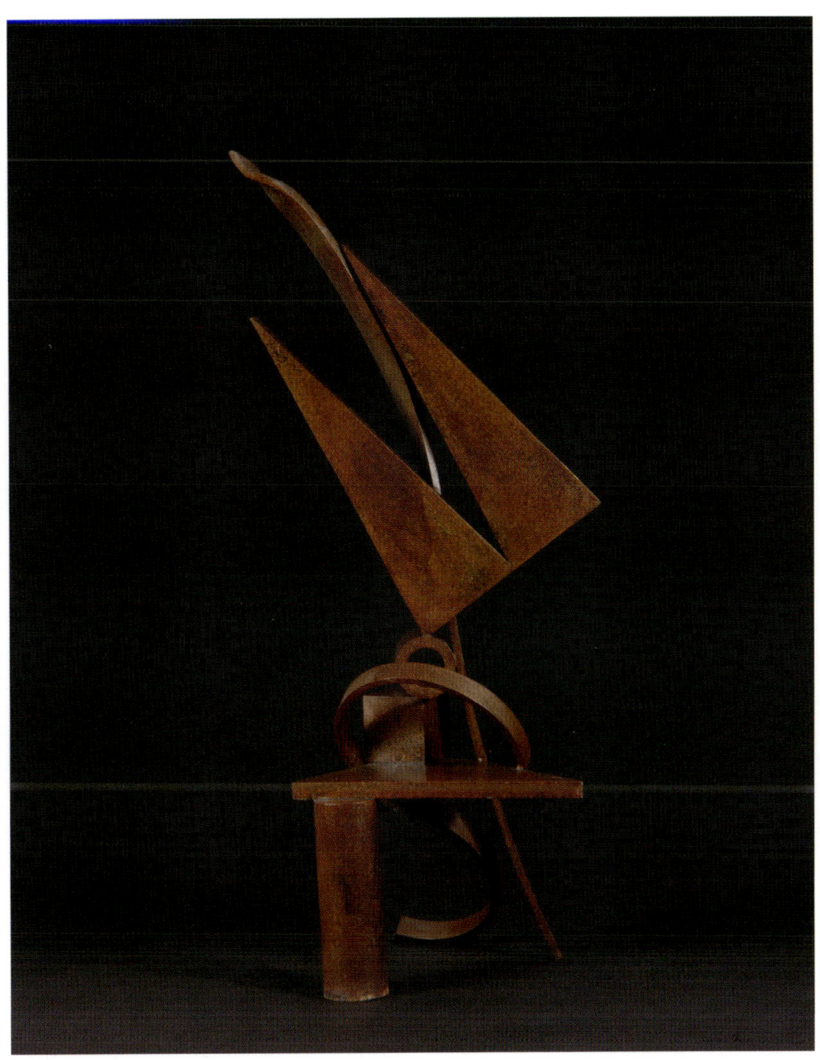

Fletcher Benton | Table 5 | 1989

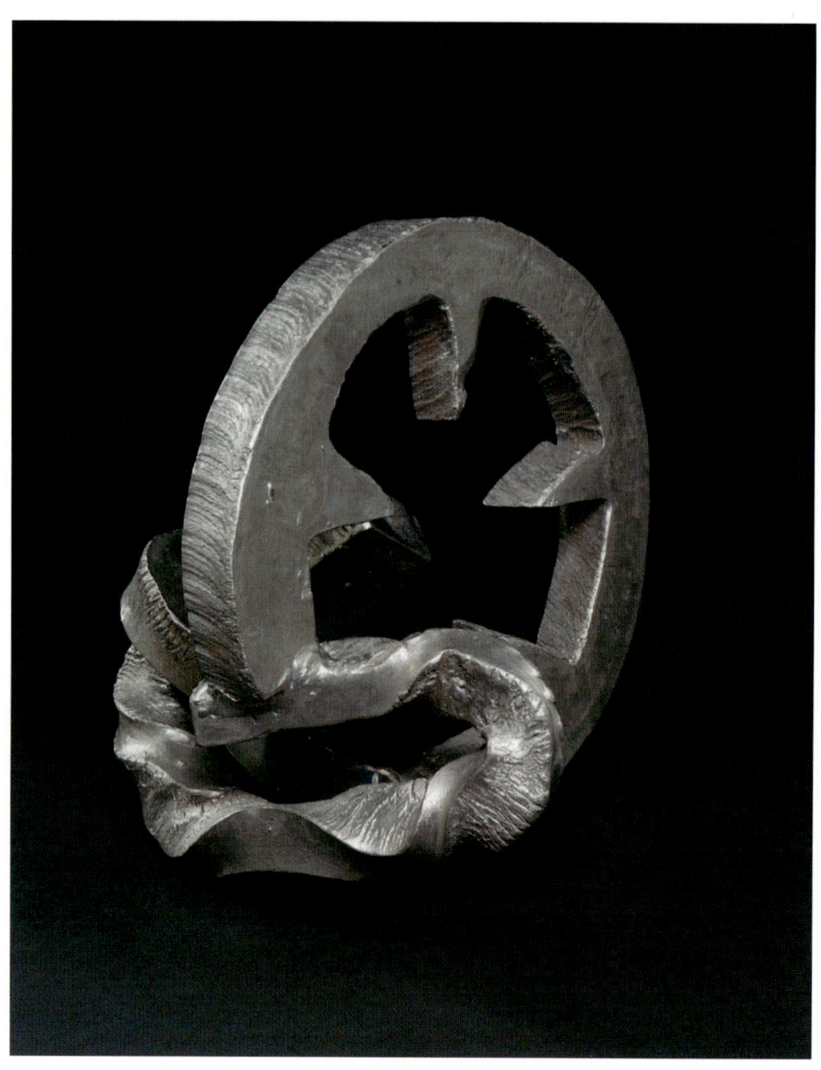

Mark di Suvero | Nukle | 2008

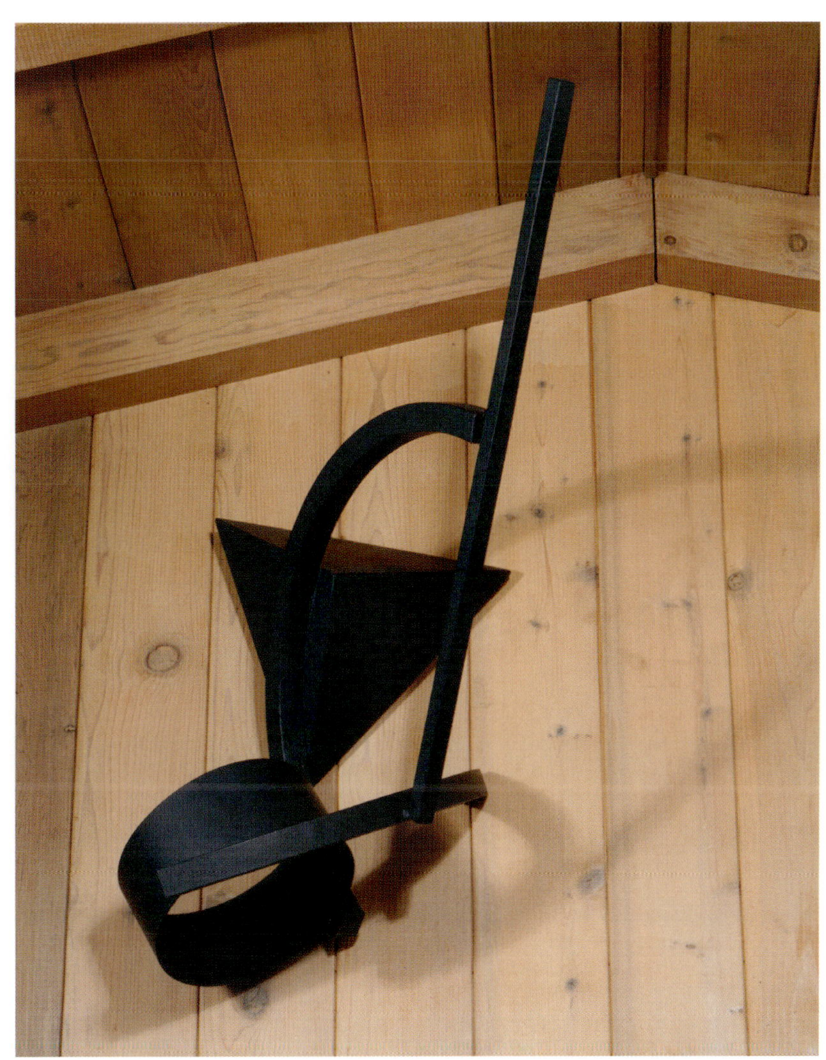

Guy Dill | Untitled Wall Sculpture | circa 1988

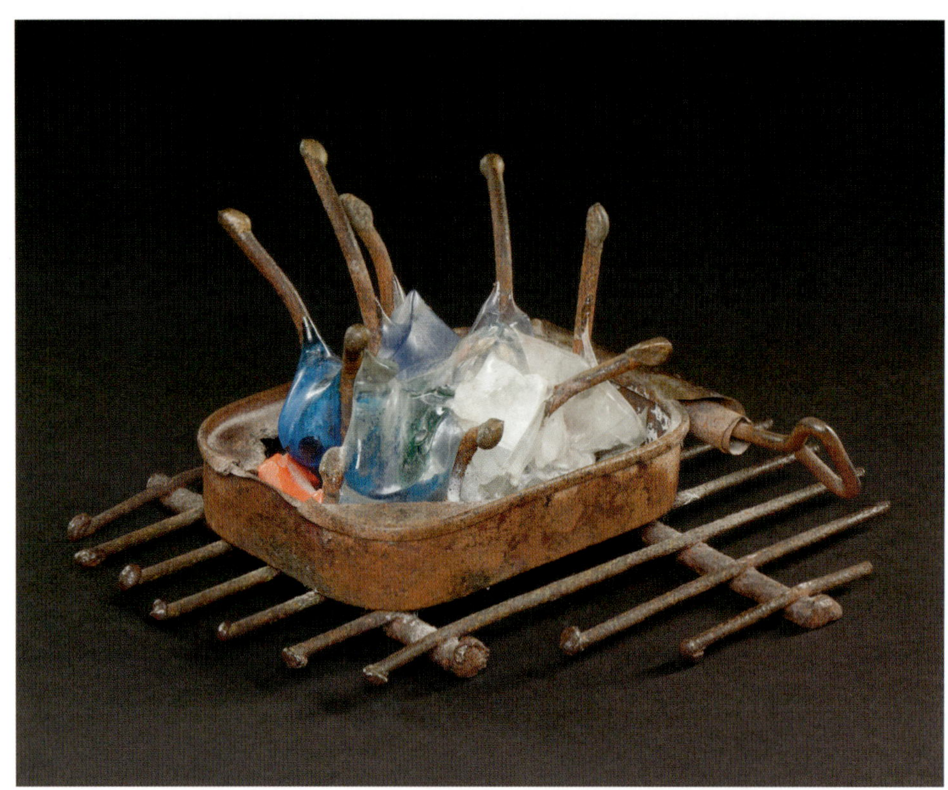

Claire Falkenstein | Untitled | circa 1960s-1970s

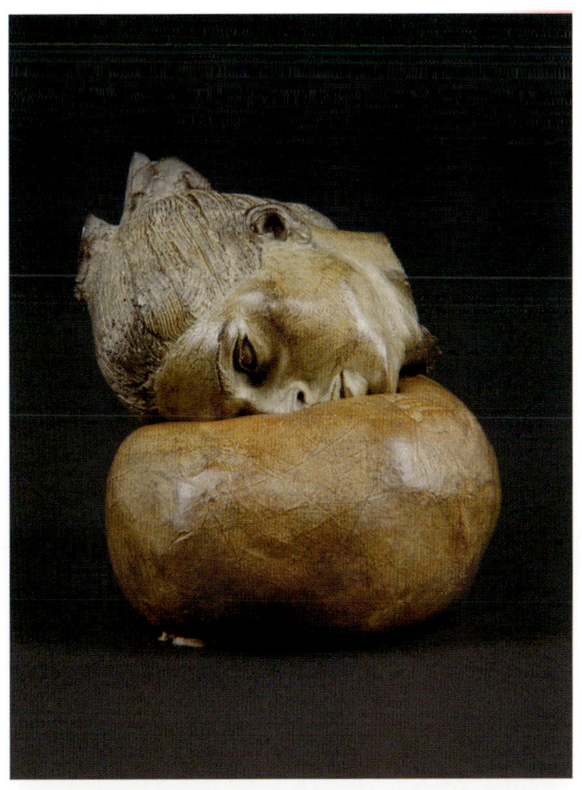

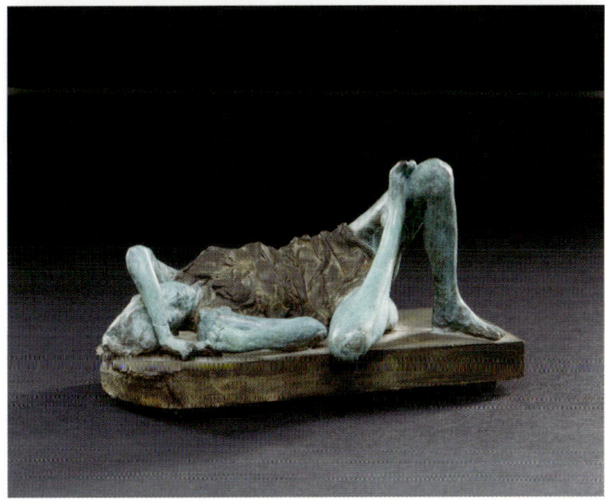

Robert Graham | Fragment Head | 1994-1995 | Elisa | 1996

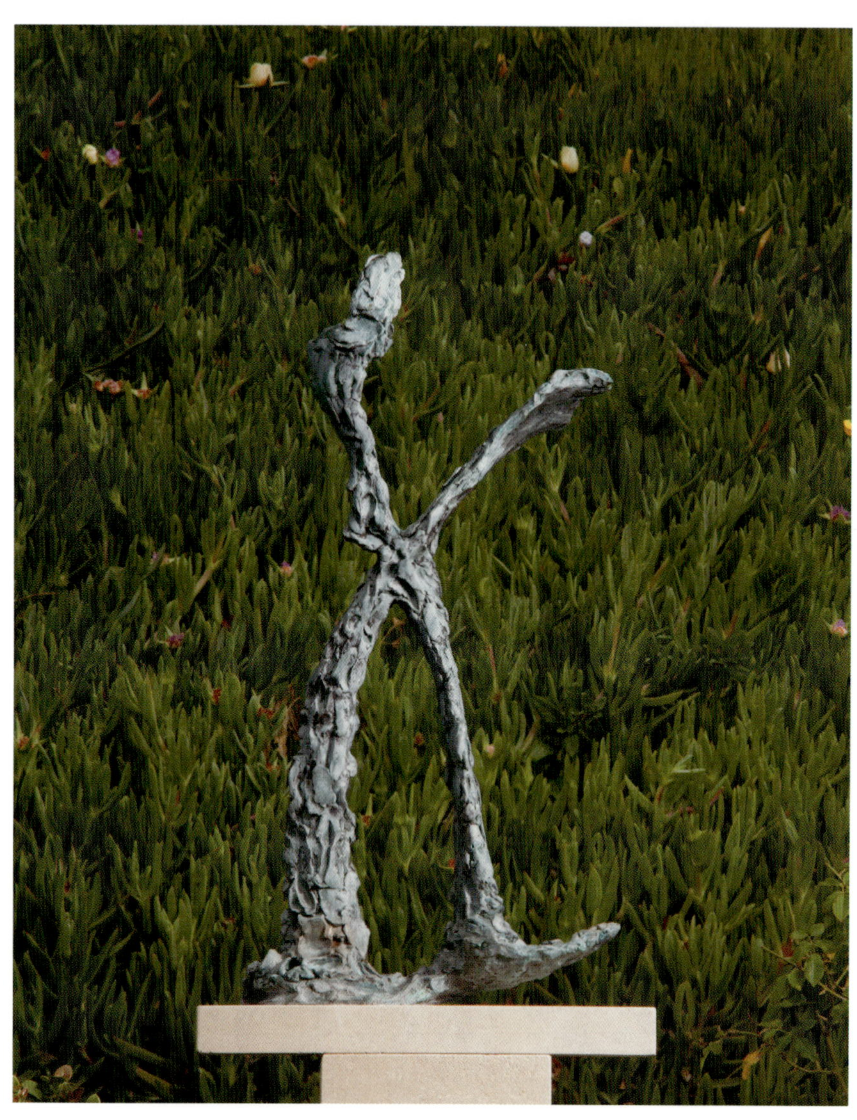

Bryan Hunt | Open Cross #2 | 1996

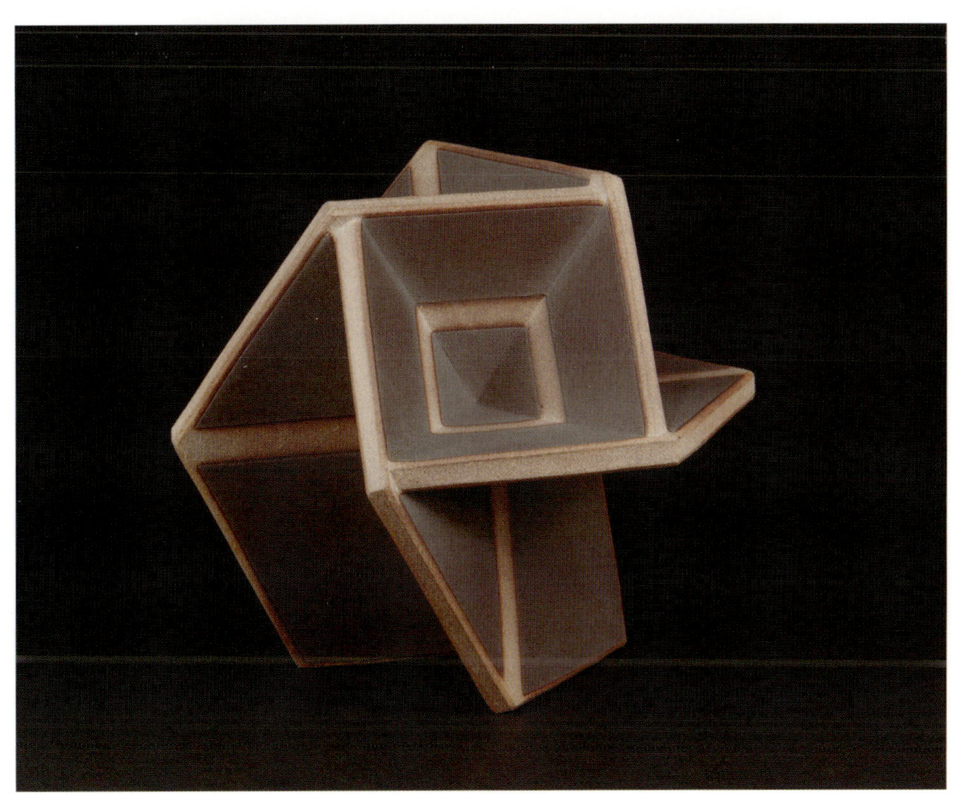

John Mason | Square Hex, Charcoal with Tracers | 2004

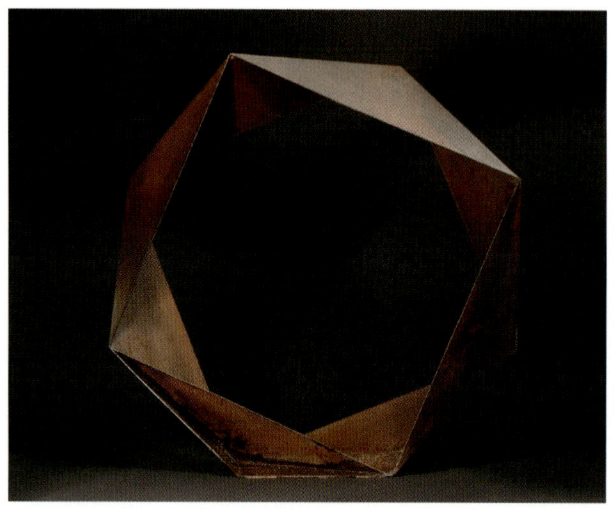

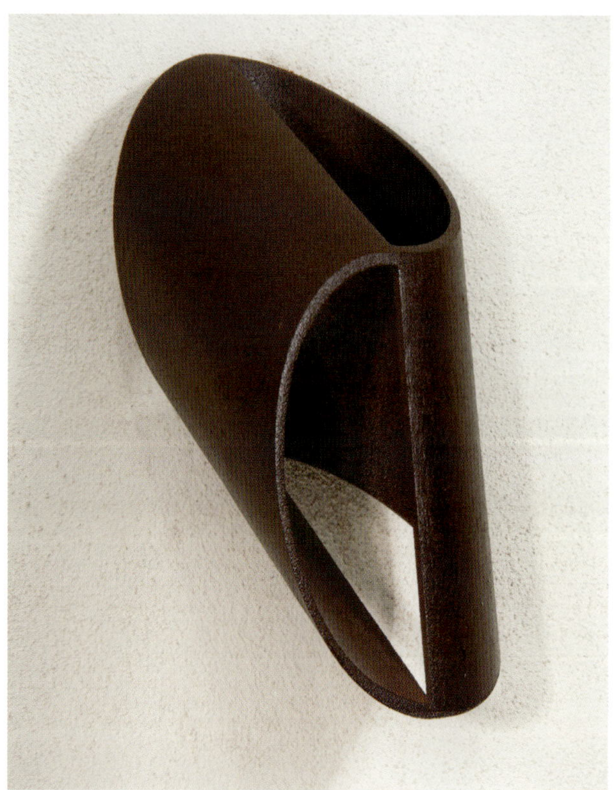

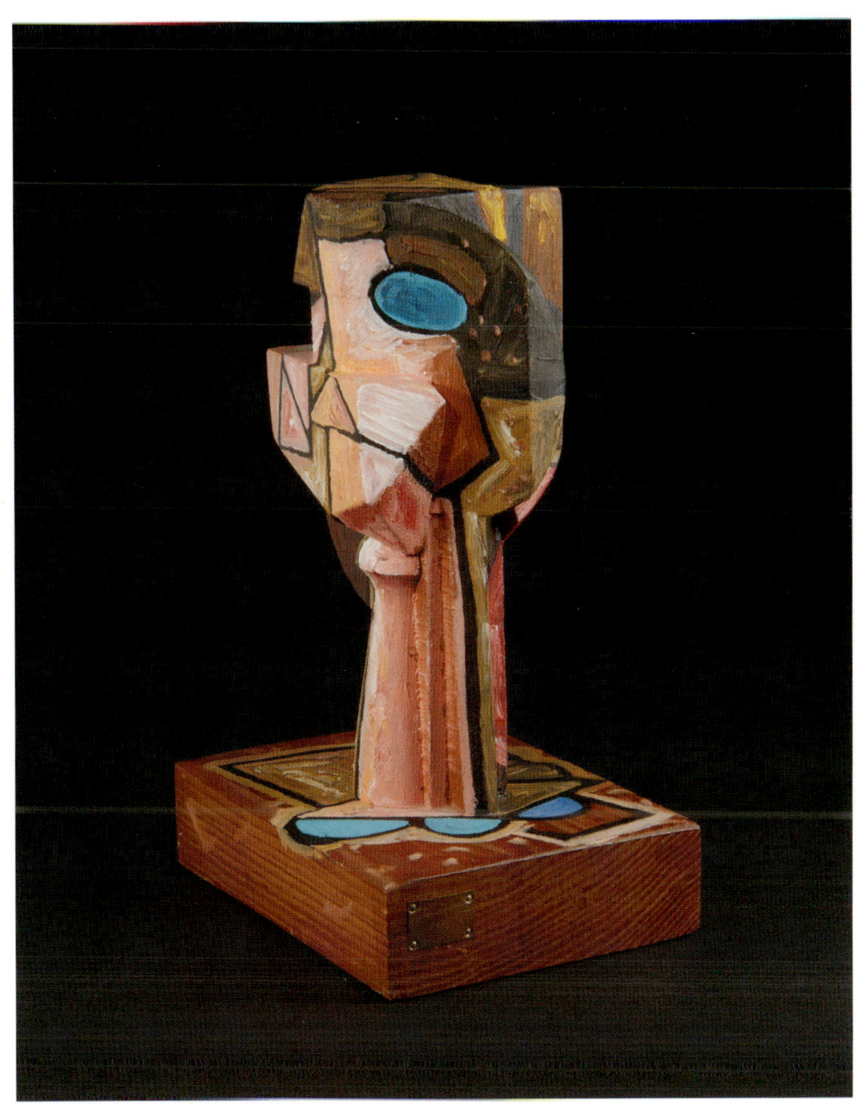

Italo Scanga | Head 78 | 1986

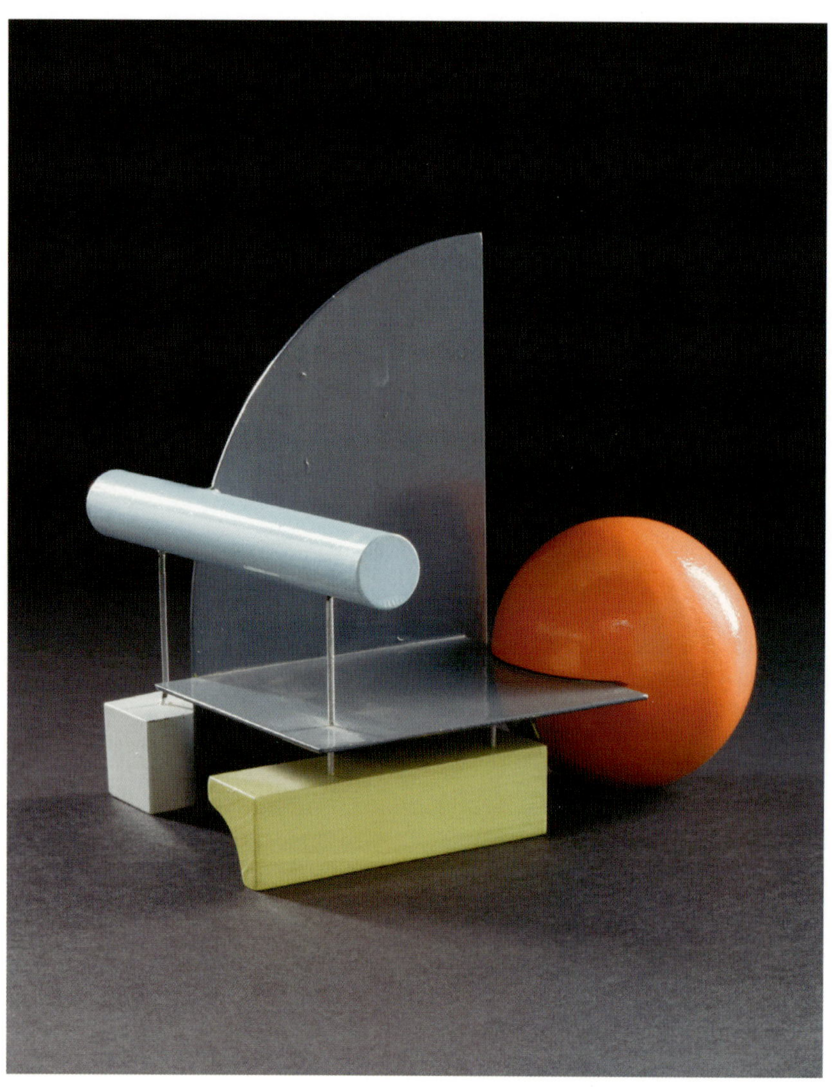

Peter Shire | Nuovo Bel Air Model | 2007

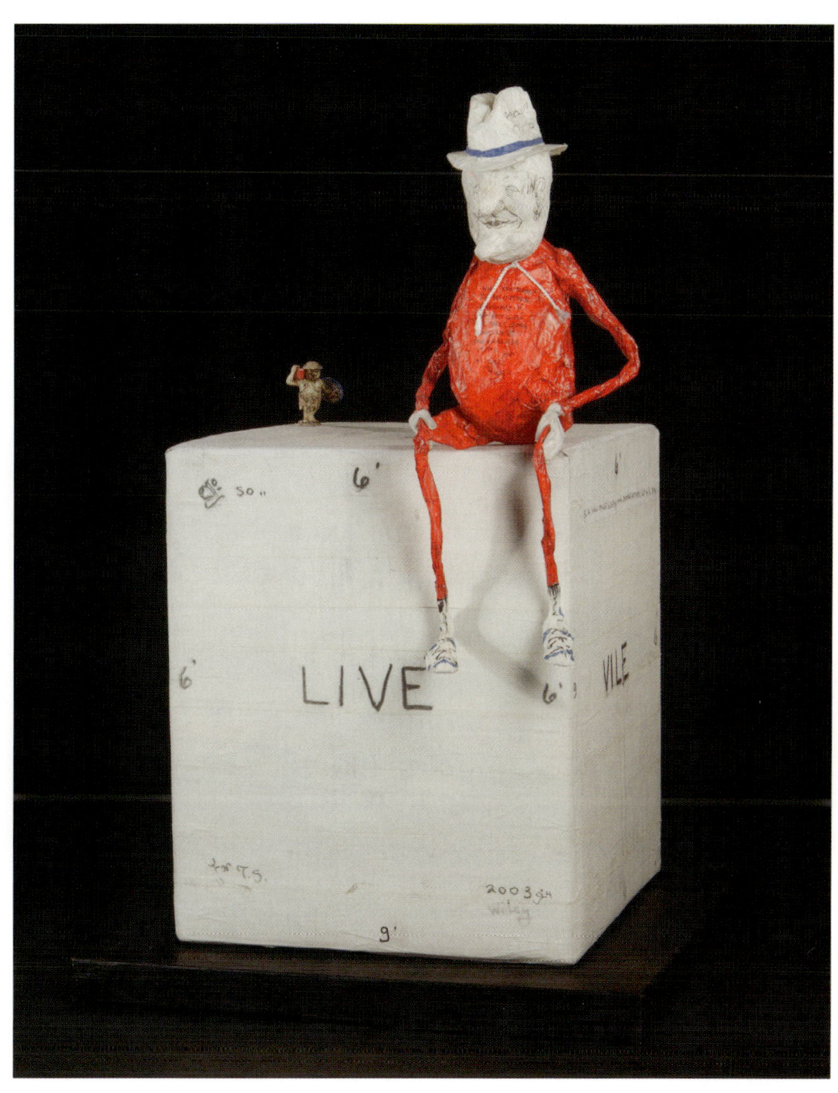

William T. Wiley | Punch Live | 2004

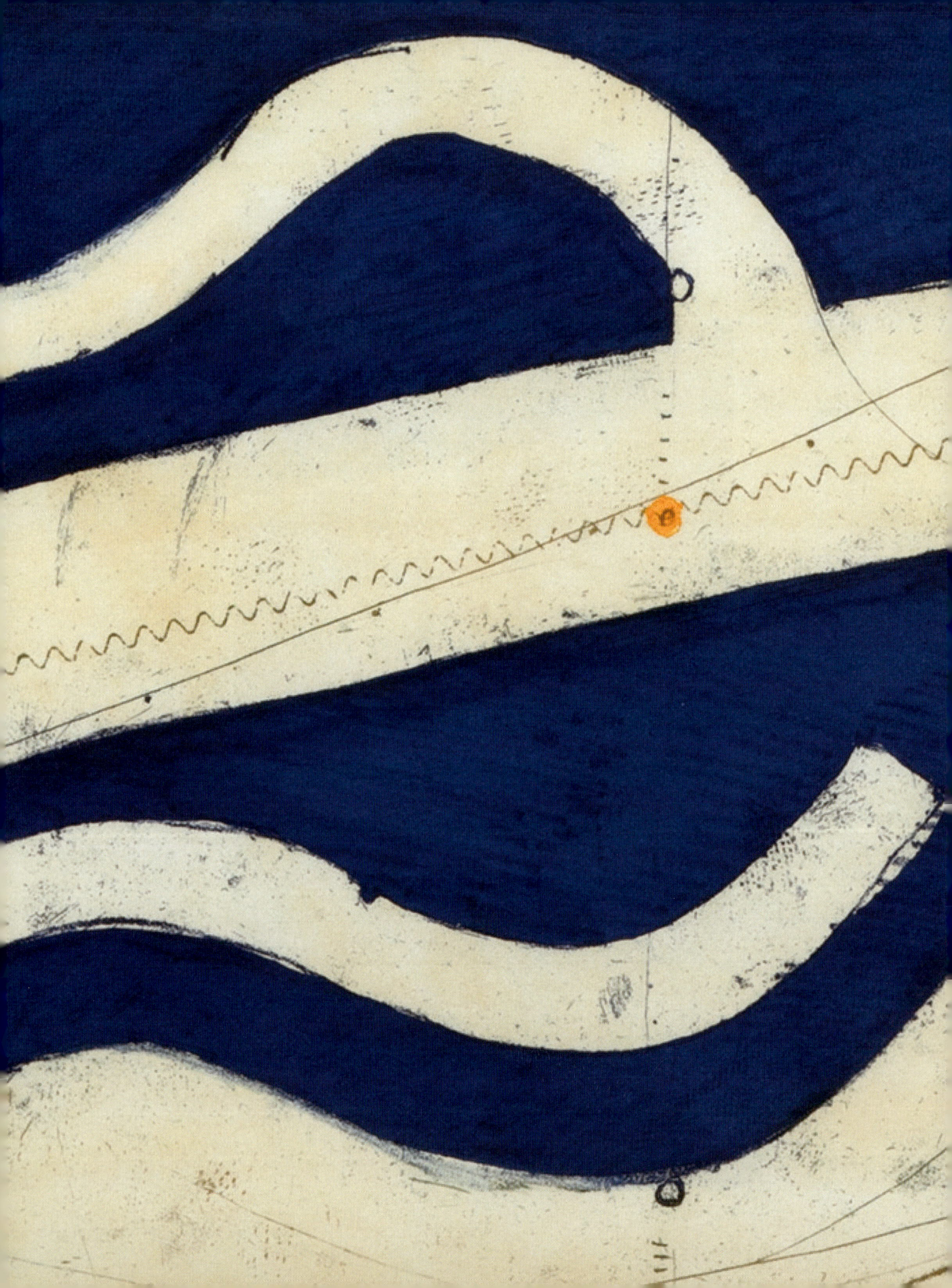

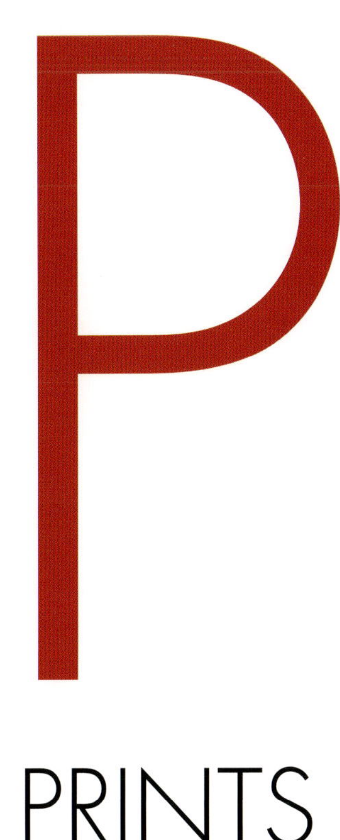

PRINTS

The prints that Wilfred Fletcher has purchased over the years constitute the most impressive section of his collection, and, consequently, are the strongest component of his latest gift to the Boise Art Museum. This group of works includes a number of artists who have made the greatest impact on post-World War II American art, and who have created some of the most fascinating works Fletcher's collection has to offer. There is, of course, good reason for this, which is Los Angeles' status as a mecca for the printmaking art form. This is due in large part to the fact that Los Angeles is home to the renowned artists' workshop and publisher of limited edition prints (and sculpture multiples) called Gemini G.E.L. Since its founding in 1966, Gemini has been the destination of more than 60 leading painters, sculptors, and other artists from all over the country eager to collaborate with the workshop's master printers in lithography, etching, screen-printing and woodcut. For a collector based in Los Angeles, it provides a goldmine of high-quality fine art.

One must also remember that concurrently throughout this period, California in general had more than its share of art schools and university art departments that helped make it a print lover's/collector's paradise. Fletcher has taken advantage of this situation to build a solid survey of contemporary American art in the print media of the last forty years.

Sam Francis, who has a substantive presence in Fletcher's holdings of California artwork, was among the first major abstract painters to make prints back in the 1950s, concentrating on lithography at Gemini after its founding. His *Handmade for Garner* from the late 70s is a rare monotype, with hand painting on paper. The piece stands out in other ways. The intense palette is certainly his, but the technique is more sinewy and tight in a Pollock-esque way than Francis' familiar splashy, floating masses. The hefty colorful gridwork underneath provides a structural foundation that is atypical for his work.

In the mid-1980s, fellow Californian Richard Diebenkorn produced a series of prints both in lithography and wood block inspired by his famous abstract paintings, such as the *Ocean Park* canvases. *Blue with Red* is a color wood block print from 1987 that contains black graphic formal elements which portend his later black and white lithographs.

Other internationally known figurative painters in the collection who have made good use of Gemini's facilities are David Hockney and Wayne Thiebaud. Hockney's prints are predominantly lithographic portraits of personal friends, an example of which was included in Fletcher's first donation to the Museum. Here, his 1981 *Big Celiaprint #1* is a much larger black and white depiction of a reclining subject rendered in an almost impressionistic style, with short daubs of ink anchored by a few broad areas of black. The result is painterly and semi-abstract.

Wayne Thiebaud's paintings of multiple, repetitive images representing the American appetite for pastries, sweets and junk food, laid out as if in a retail display, established his reputation as a leading figure of the Pop movement, and also made perfect subjects for color lithography, which he started exploring in the 1960s. During his career, his subjects would expand to include all sorts of fashion items and commodities, as well as cityscapes and urban scenes. His 1990 multi-colored lithograph *Bow Ties*, depicting rows of differently patterned ties as you might see them in the men's department at Macy's, is a classic example of the Pop sensibility underlying so much of his art.

Jim Dine is another pioneer in the cult of the object, although his connection with Pop is more tenuous. He enjoys and contributes to the paradoxical in contemporary American art, but his resourcefulness with a range of materials and an idiosyncratic expressionistic, neo-Dadaist style set him apart from Pop artists. His first mentor was Jasper Johns, whose influence is demonstrated in Dine's works that comprise a series of images or symbols. *Hammer with Watercolors*, from 1982, is a valentine of violence made of repeating heart shapes in the midst of which lurks a potentially dangerous hammer. Dine has never been a fan of sentimentality.

Demonstrating Gemini's ability to attract some of the most prominent artists of the day, Jasper Johns himself collaborated with the workshop beginning in the 1960s to publish landmark lithographs based on his *Numerical Series*. Johns had a keen sensibility to the unique nature of print media surfaces, as shown in the later tonal wash renderings of his *0 through 9* series printed on gray paper. The unique 1975 intaglio aquatint etching, *0*, that Fletcher acquired reveals the delicate subtleties Johns was able to achieve in print.

Other well known East Coast painters of the era who delved into printmaking and are represented in this collection are Helen Frankenthaler and Ellsworth Kelly. Frankenthaler was influenced by Jackson Pollock, which in some ways is more evident in her prints than her paintings. On canvas she became known for her stain painting technique, applying light-colored pigments onto primed canvas, thereby integrating color and support. (Critic Clement Greenberg named it "post-painterly abstraction," and it would influence such artists as Morris Louis.) The two prints donated by Fletcher combine color etching, mezzotint, aquatint and pochoir in abstract compositions that integrate a watercolor-like palette with a curvilinear drawing technique reminiscent of Pollock's early paintings.

The intelligent, persistently independent painter and sculptor Ellsworth Kelly has proven a major printmaker as well. Since 1970, Kelly has published over 250 lithographs, screenprints, aquatints and etchings at Gemini. His abstract works appear non-objective but in a very basic sense are not. They articulate the nature of form by referencing its physical nature, i.e., scale, weight, color, depth, shape, edge and mass. The intensity of his imagery, as in his color lithograph *Blue* (one of two pieces in this donation) is largely due to the literalness he brings to abstraction via nature- and architecture-derived forms. An undeniable influence on minimalism, color field and hard-edge painting, post-painterly abstraction, and Op Art, Kelly nevertheless managed to stand apart from them.

Another innovator in the aesthetics of abstract form is the sculptor and printmaker Richard Serra, who continues to have an enormous presence in contemporary American art. His monumental steel sculptures investigate the ways the work, the viewer, and the territory interact, especially in forms in which the curved metal tilts on its axial plane. Serra has also been collaborating with Gemini since 1972, exploring isolated black shapes in various media.

As a printmaker, Serra is an expert at visualizing sculptural properties of weight, gravity, balance, and the often precarious moment of their intersection. Case in point is his lithograph from 1972, *Circuit*. The vortex of the imposing, converging planes pulls us in, but not without hesitation on our part. This is not an image of clean delineations but rather of industrial shop grit and a work in process. It recalls his much earlier work where he would splash molten lead against the corners of gallery walls, in the process obscuring the meeting points of floor and wall, wall and adjacent wall. Dark and dense, *Circuit* conjures his once-expressed desire to achieve "the discrete object dissolved into the sculptural field." [1]

Serra's 6-panel black etchings on white paper that constitute his 2003 *The Line of the Curve* are an Ellsworth Kellyian exercise in contemplation of a particular form, in this case individual variations on the curve and its suggestiveness. A distillation of Serra's art, they provide a fascinating insight into the building blocks of his dynamic formal vocabulary.

The Museum is also extremely fortunate to be the recipient, once again, of prints by Robert Motherwell, who excels in the printmaking art form. Originally a student of philosophy, literature, criticism and art history at Stanford and at Columbia, in New York, Motherwell hung out with the exiled French surrealists who congregated there. Under their influence he developed his own post-surrealist style, entwining free association or automatism and an innate sense of form and order, an aesthetic particularly prominent in his print works. Both his *Alberti Elegy* and the *Beau Geste I* lithographs harken back to the existential, organic black and white *Elegies* which movingly embodied his concept of "ordered chaos."

The inclusion of other important American abstractionists like Sol LeWitt, Jun Kaneko and Terry Winters, along with the figurative artist Alex Katz, in this gift, further establishes the print portion as the backbone of Fletcher's collection.

[1] Richard Serra, "Rigging" (1980) in Kristine Stiles and Peter Selz, *Theories and Documents of Contemporary Art: A Sourcebook of Artists' Writings* (Berkeley and Los Angeles, University of California Press, 1996), 601.

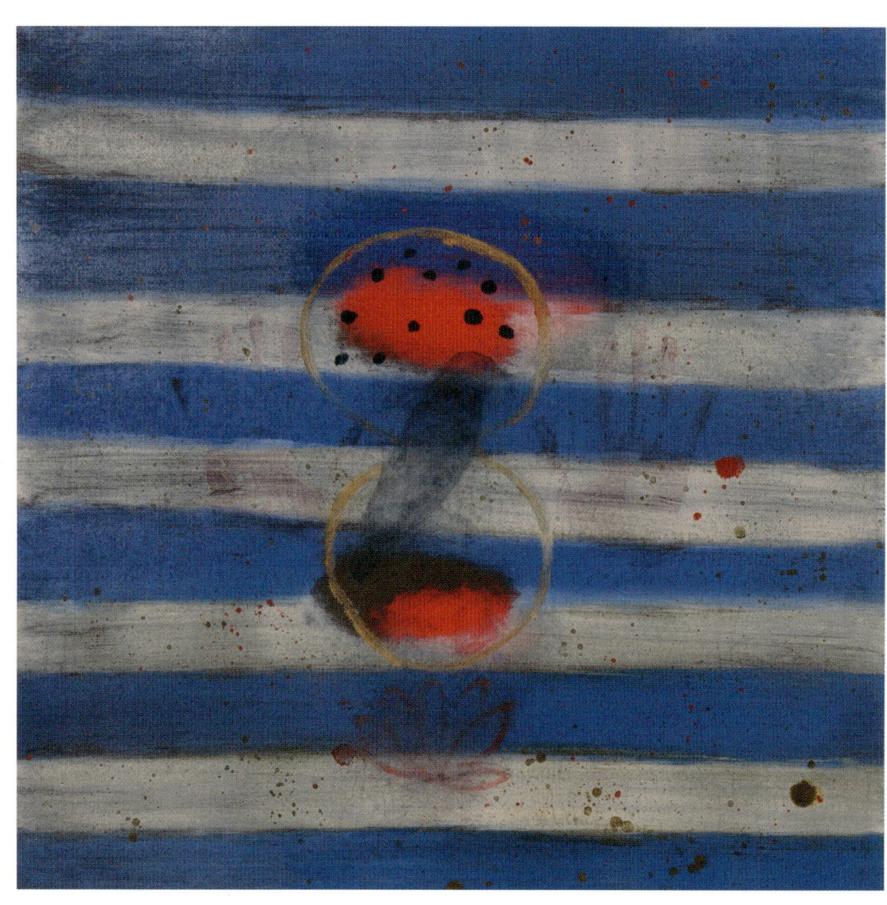

Squeak Carnwath | Untitled | 1991

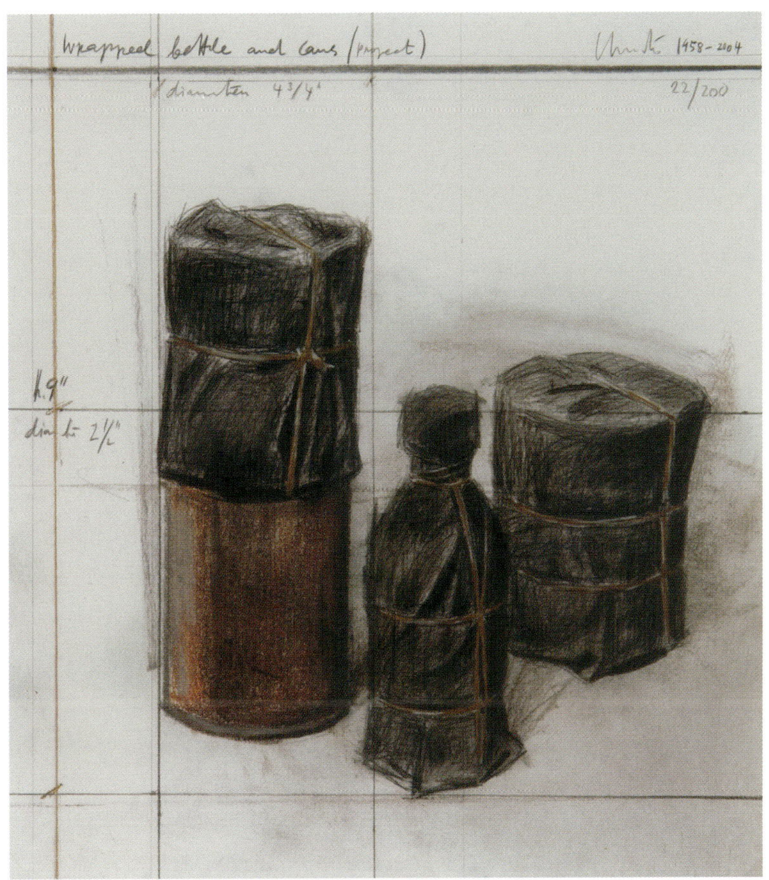

Christo | Wrapped Bottle and Cans (Project) | 1958-2004

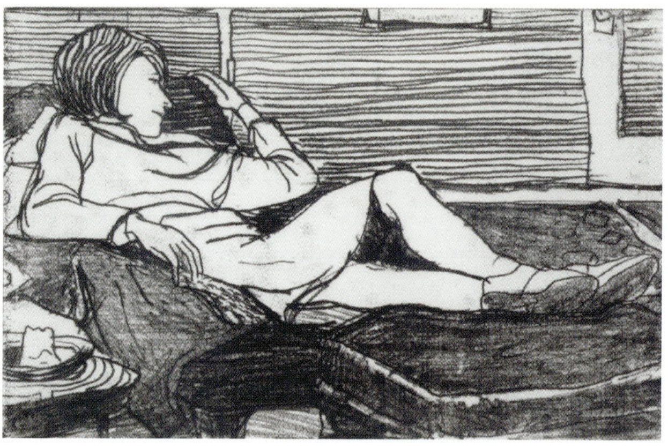

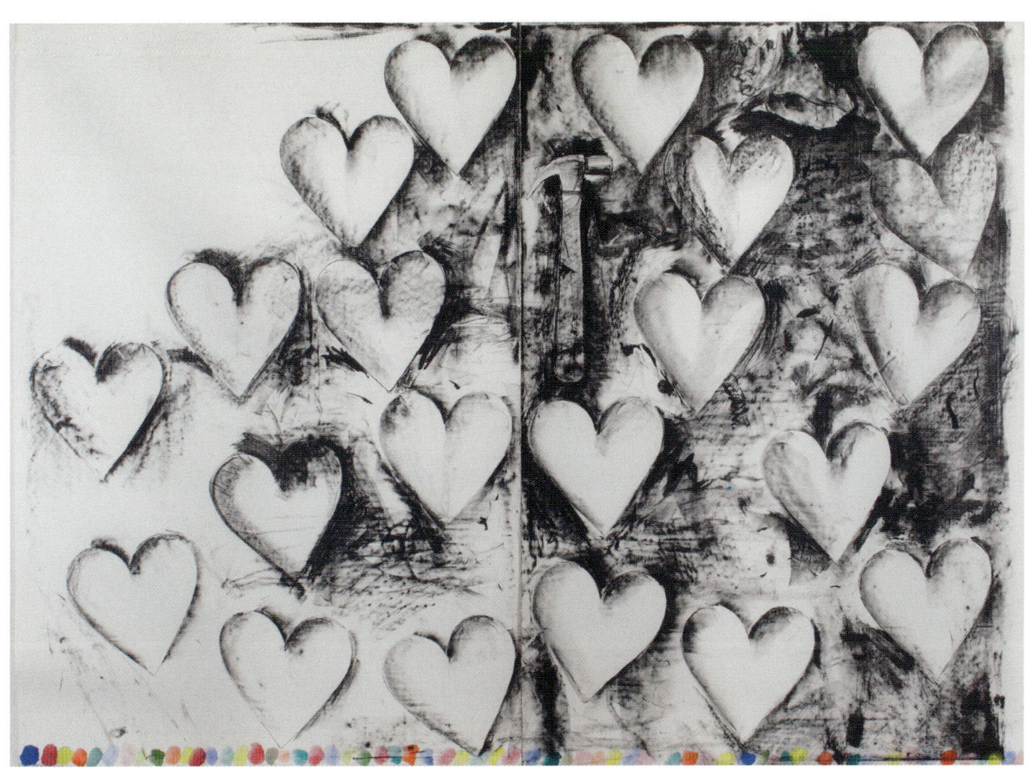

Jim Dine | Hammer with Watercolors | 1992

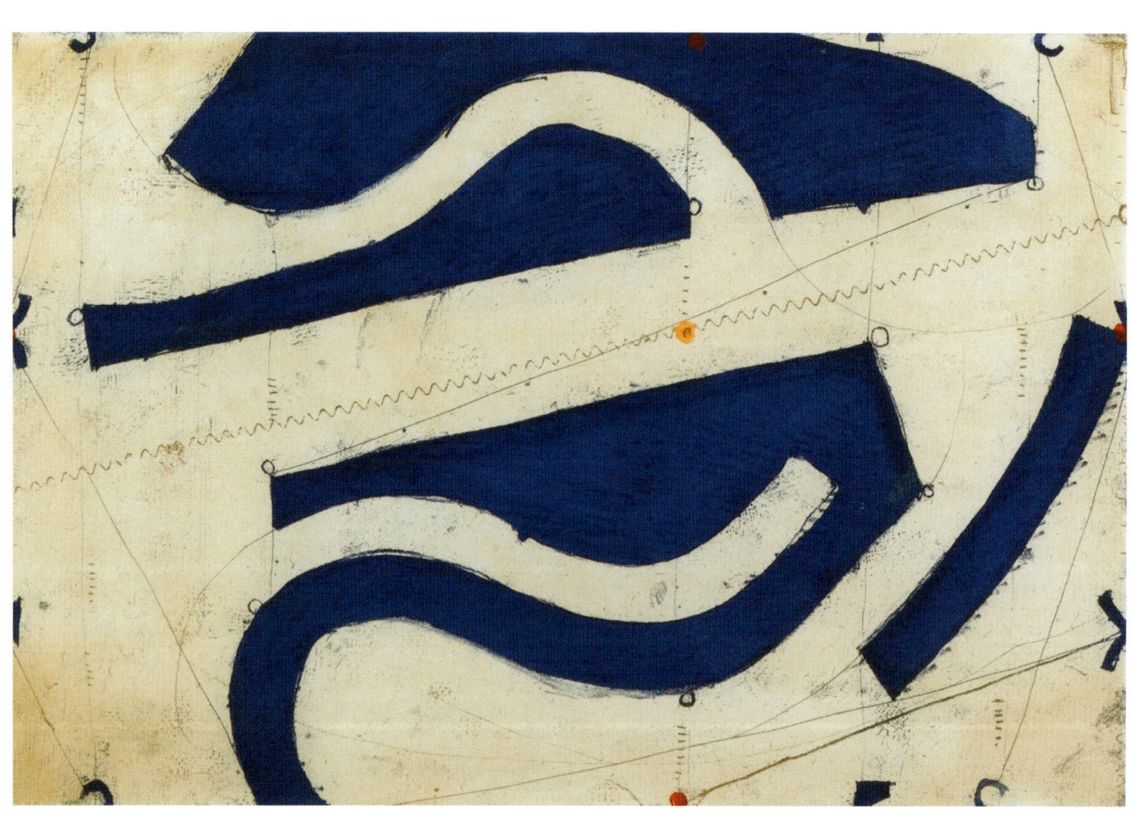

Caio Fonseca | Little Fifth | 1999

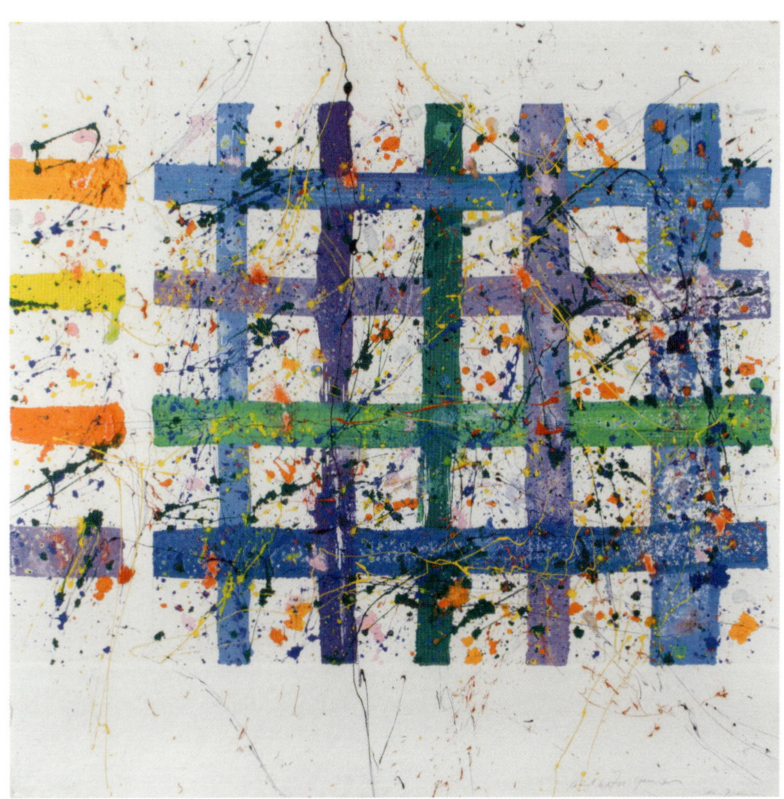

Sam Francis | Handmade for Garner | late 1970s

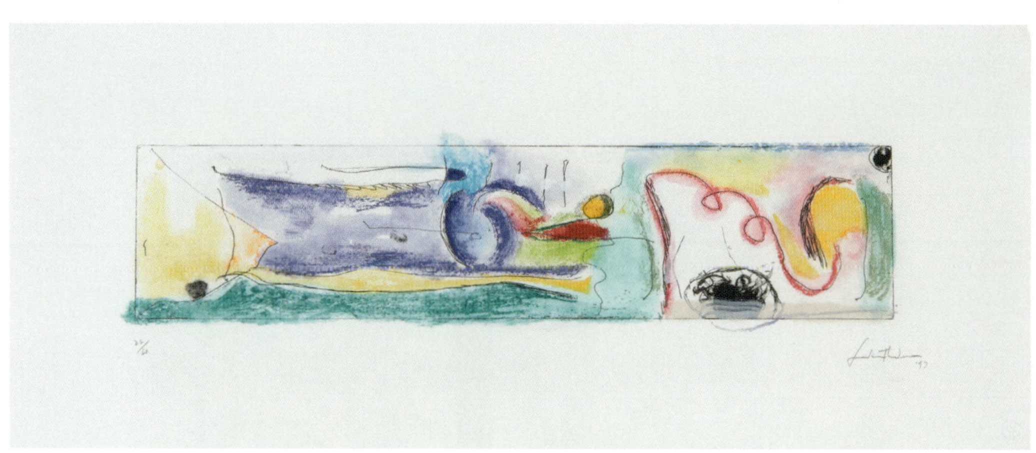

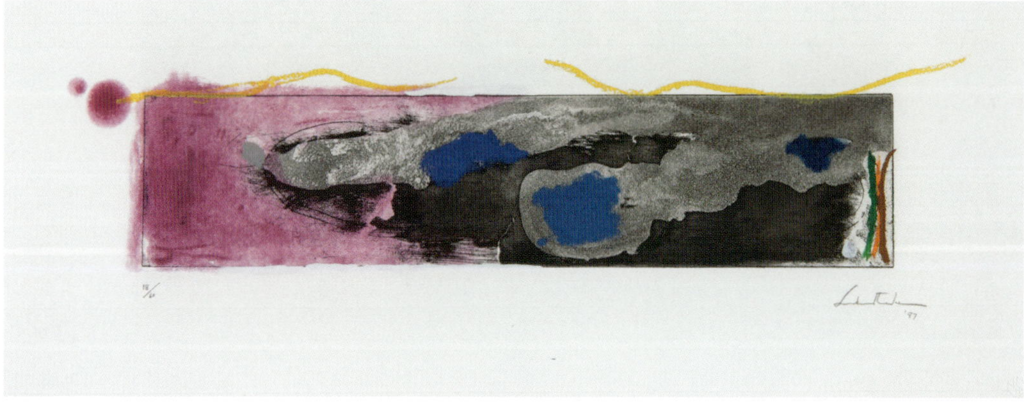

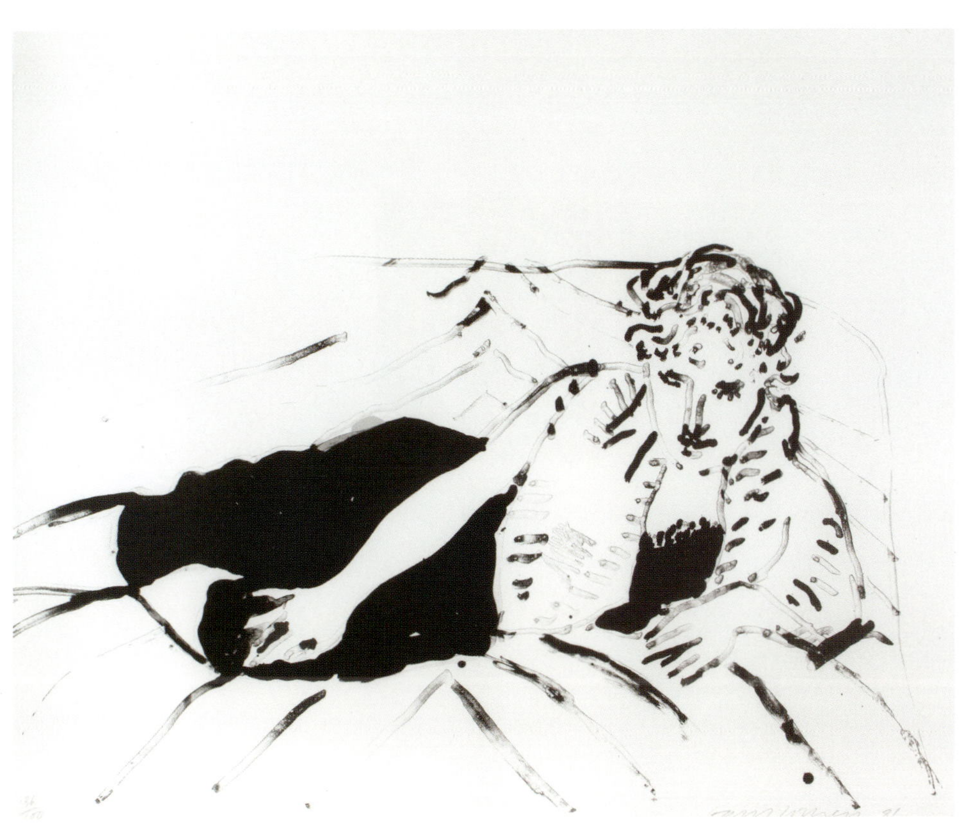

David Hockney | Big Celiaprint #1 | 1981

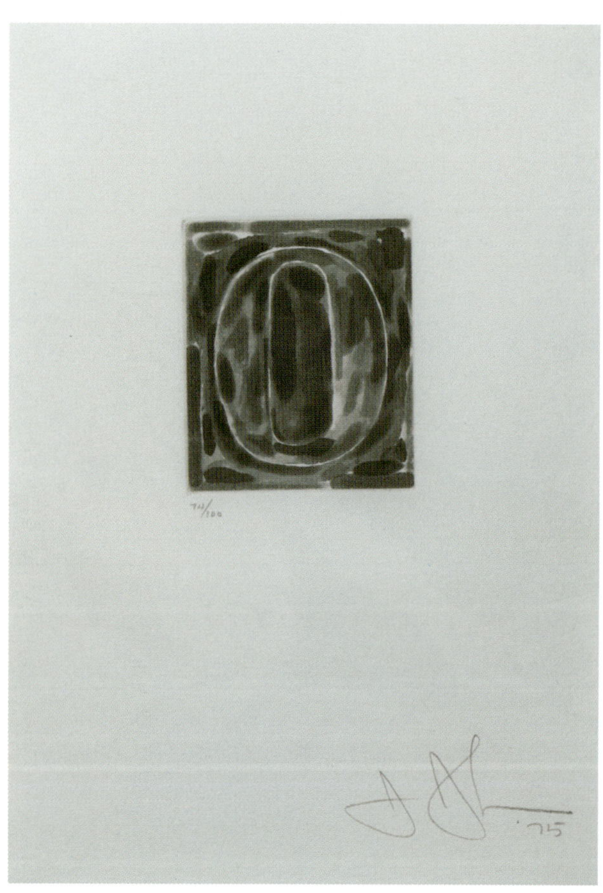

Jasper Johns | 0 (Zero) | 1975

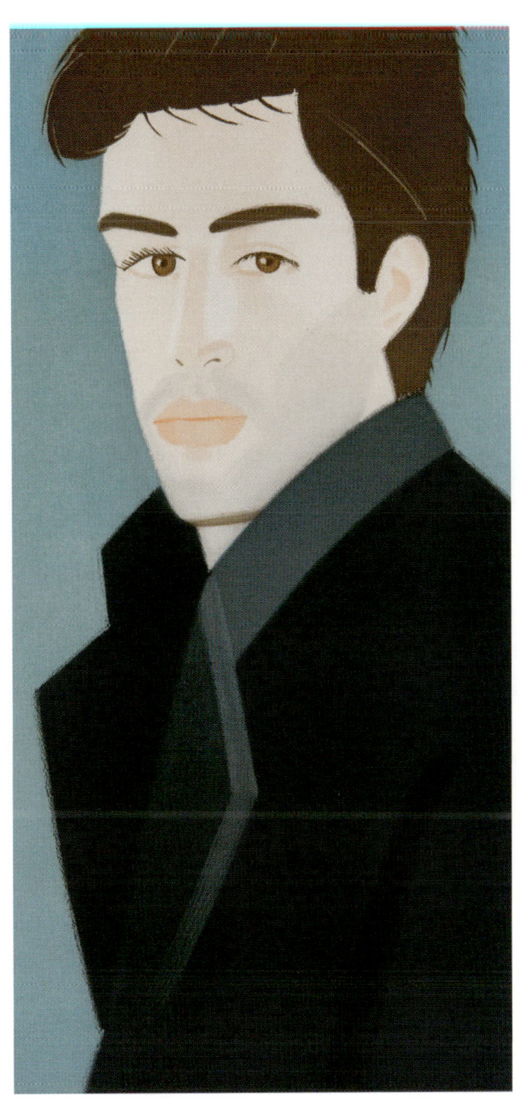

Alex Katz | Vincent | 1993

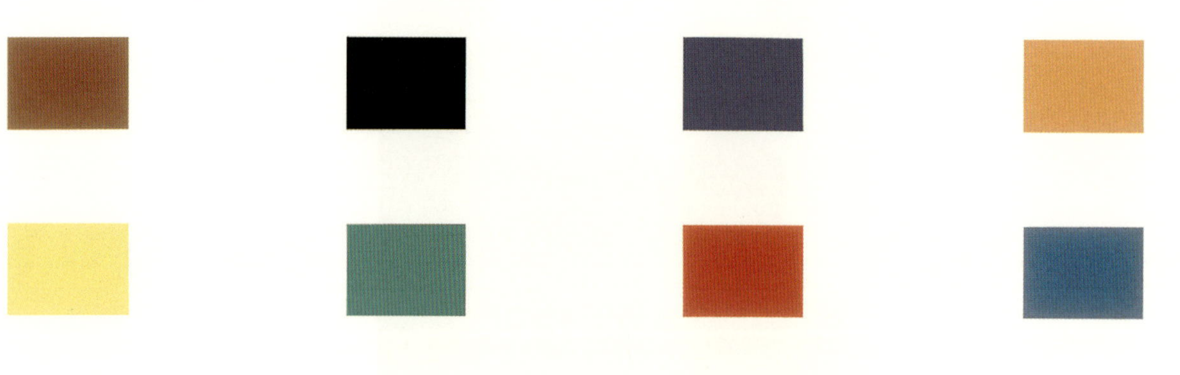

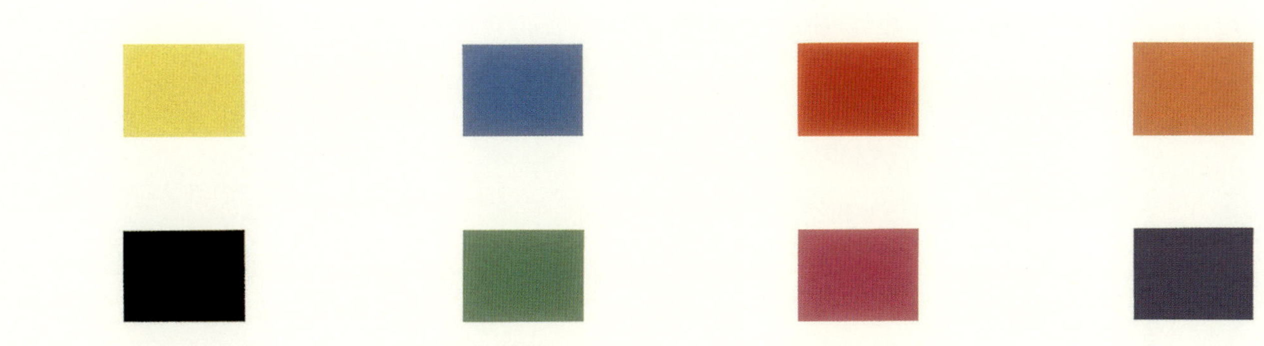

Ellsworth Kelly | 18 Colors (Cincinnati) | 1979-1982

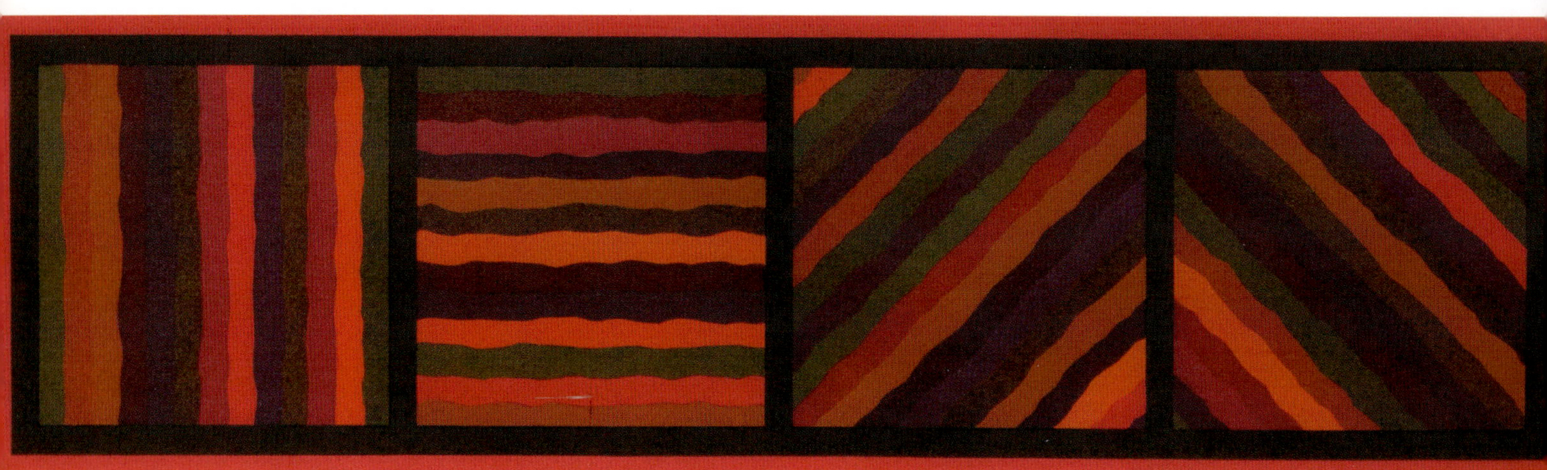

Sol LeWitt | Bands (Not Straight) in Four Directions - Red | 1999

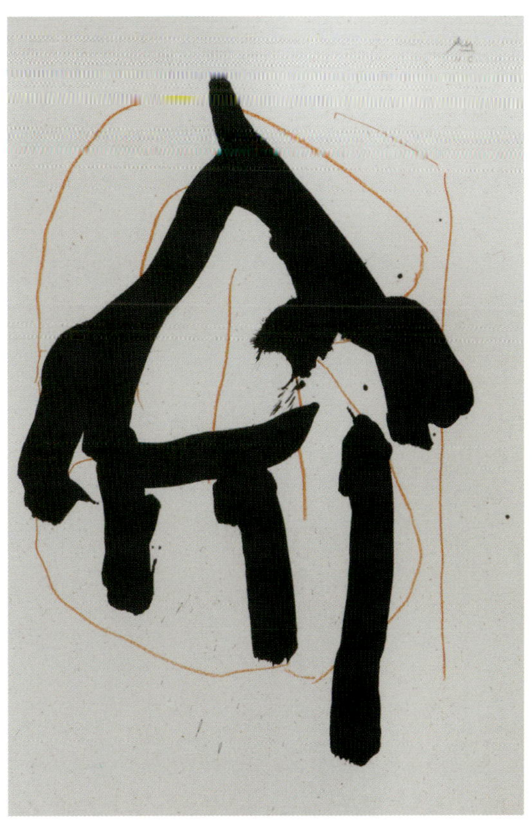

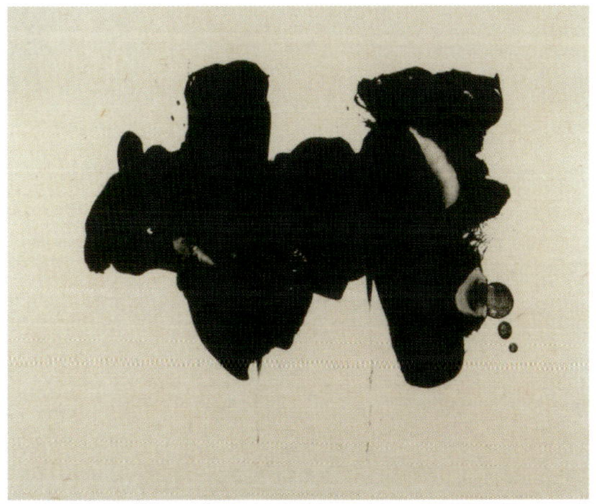

Robert Motherwell | Beau Geste I | 1989 | Alberti Elegy |1982

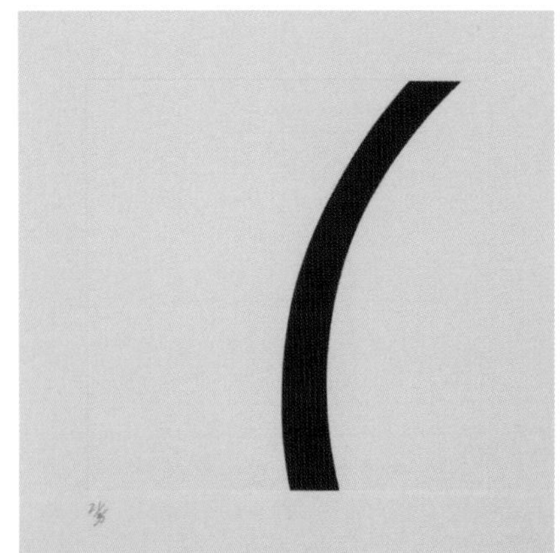 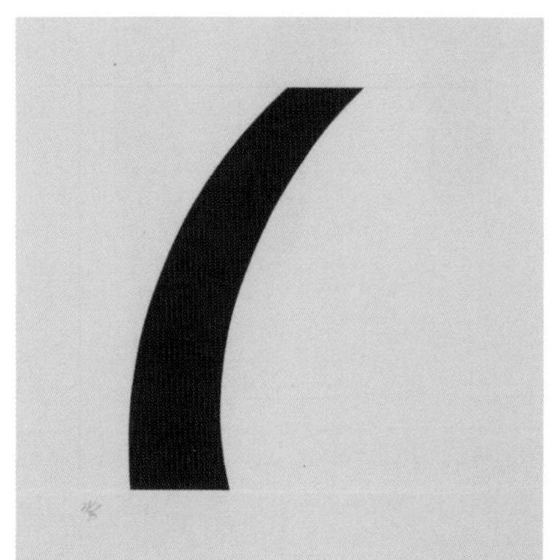 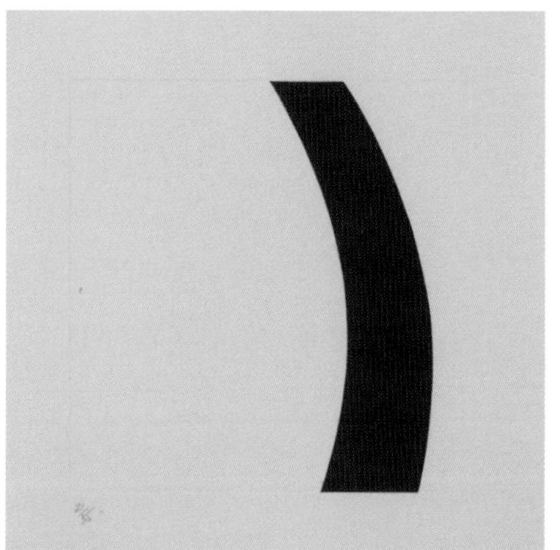

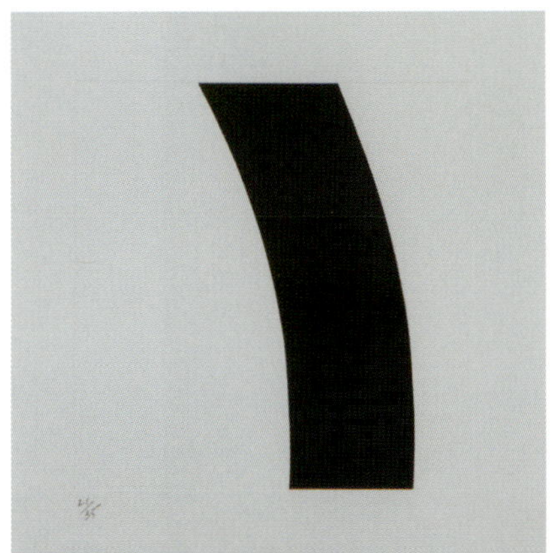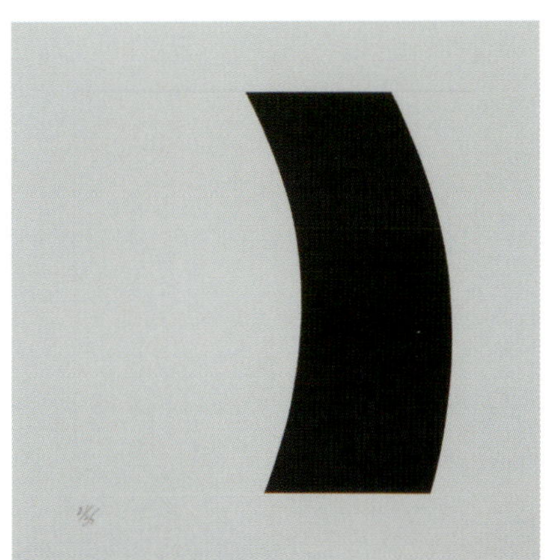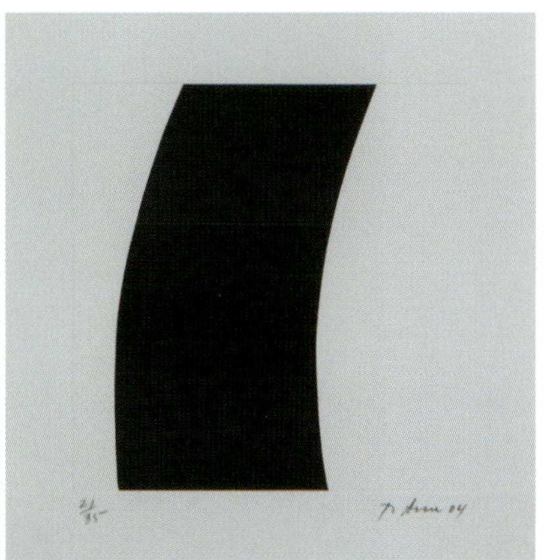

Richard Serra | The Line of the Curve | 2004

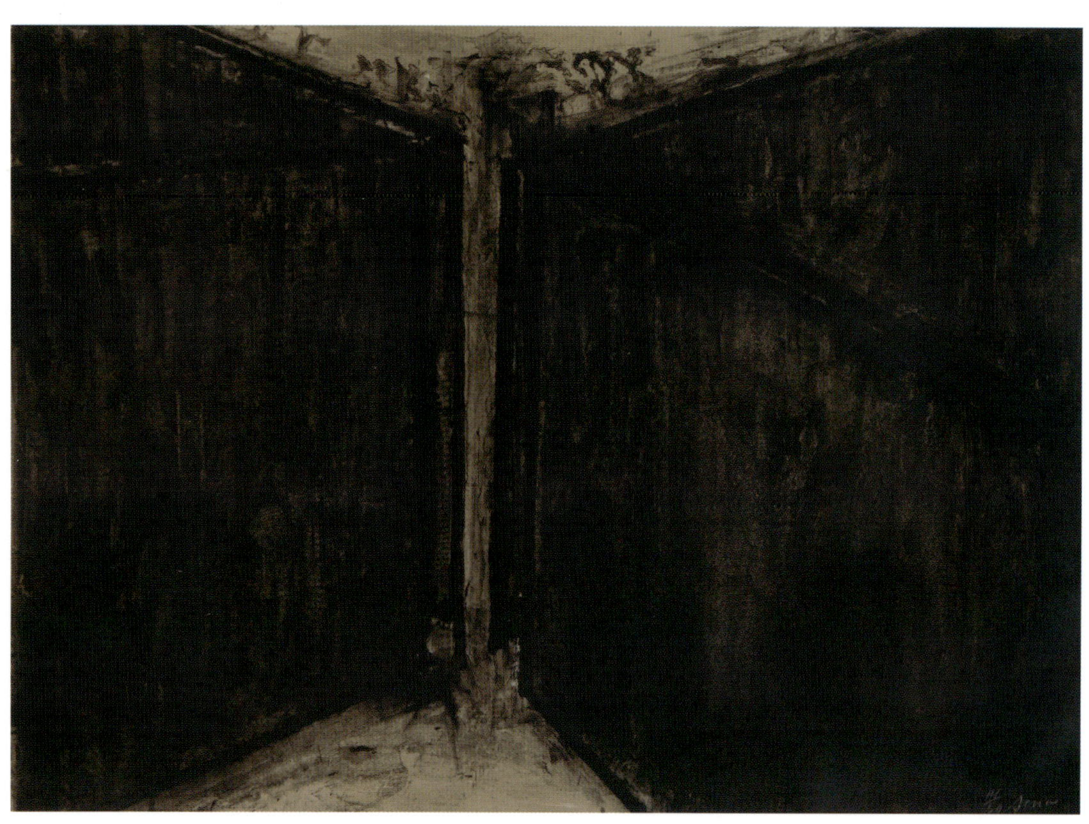

Richard Serra | Circuit | 1972

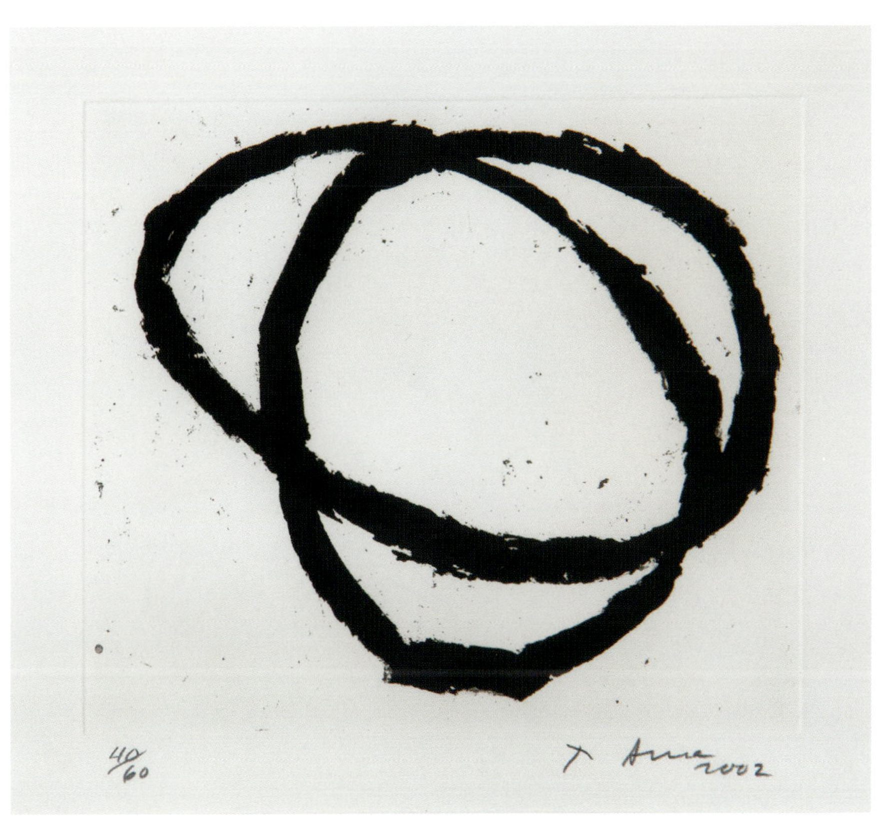

Richard Serra | Venice Notebook 2001, #1 | 2002

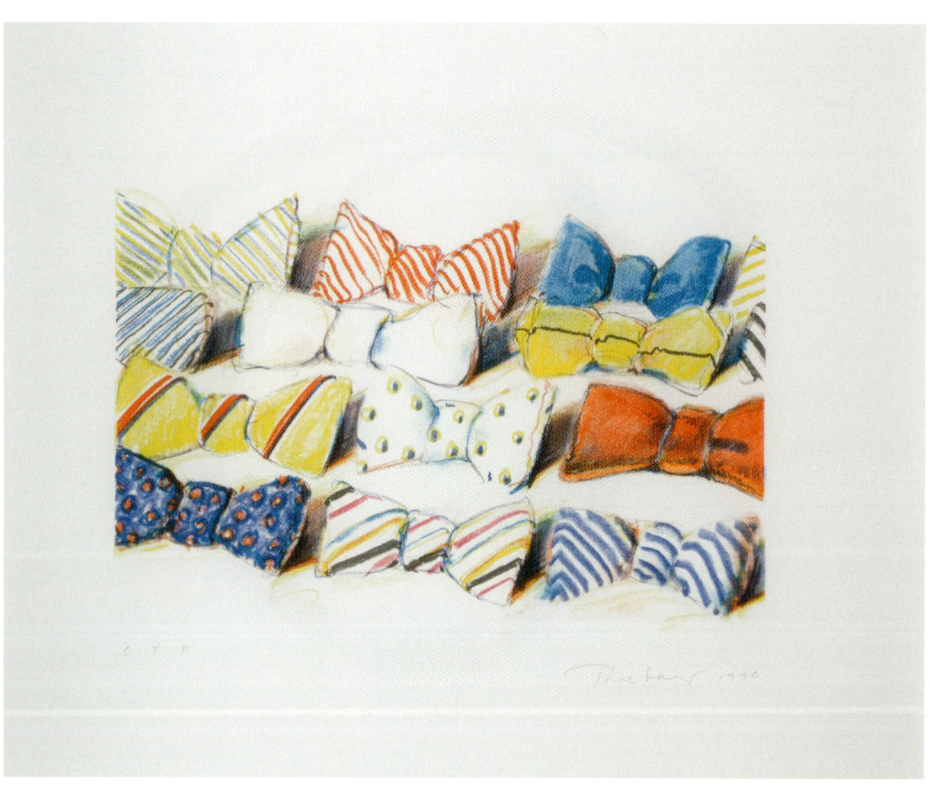

Wayne Thiebaud | Bow Ties |1990

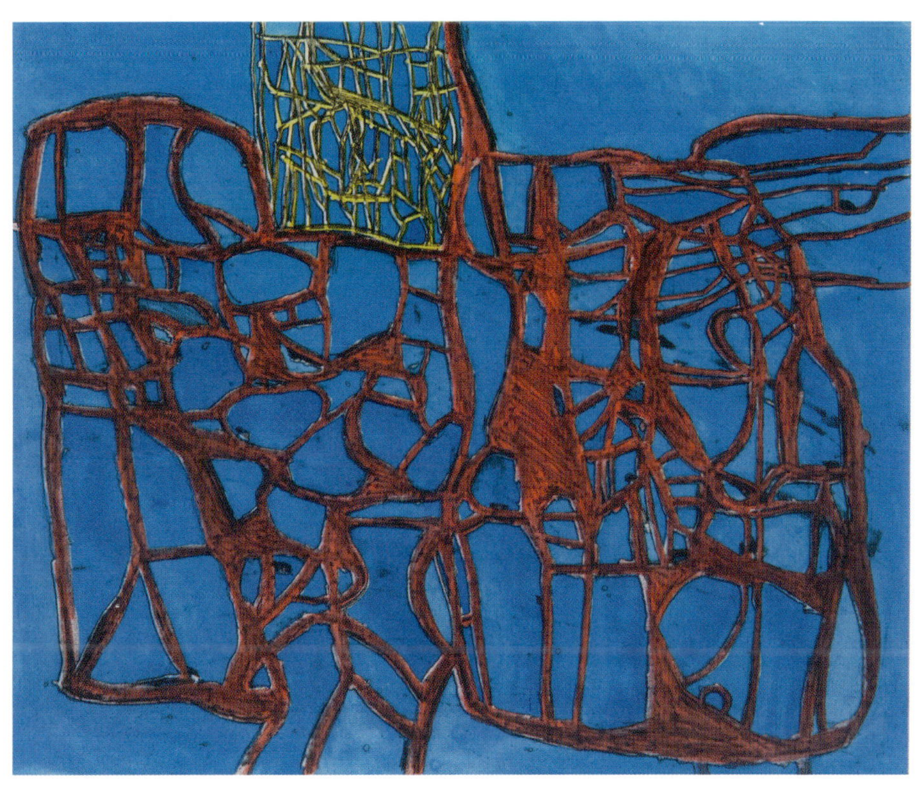

Terry Winters | Models for Synthetic Pictures | 1994

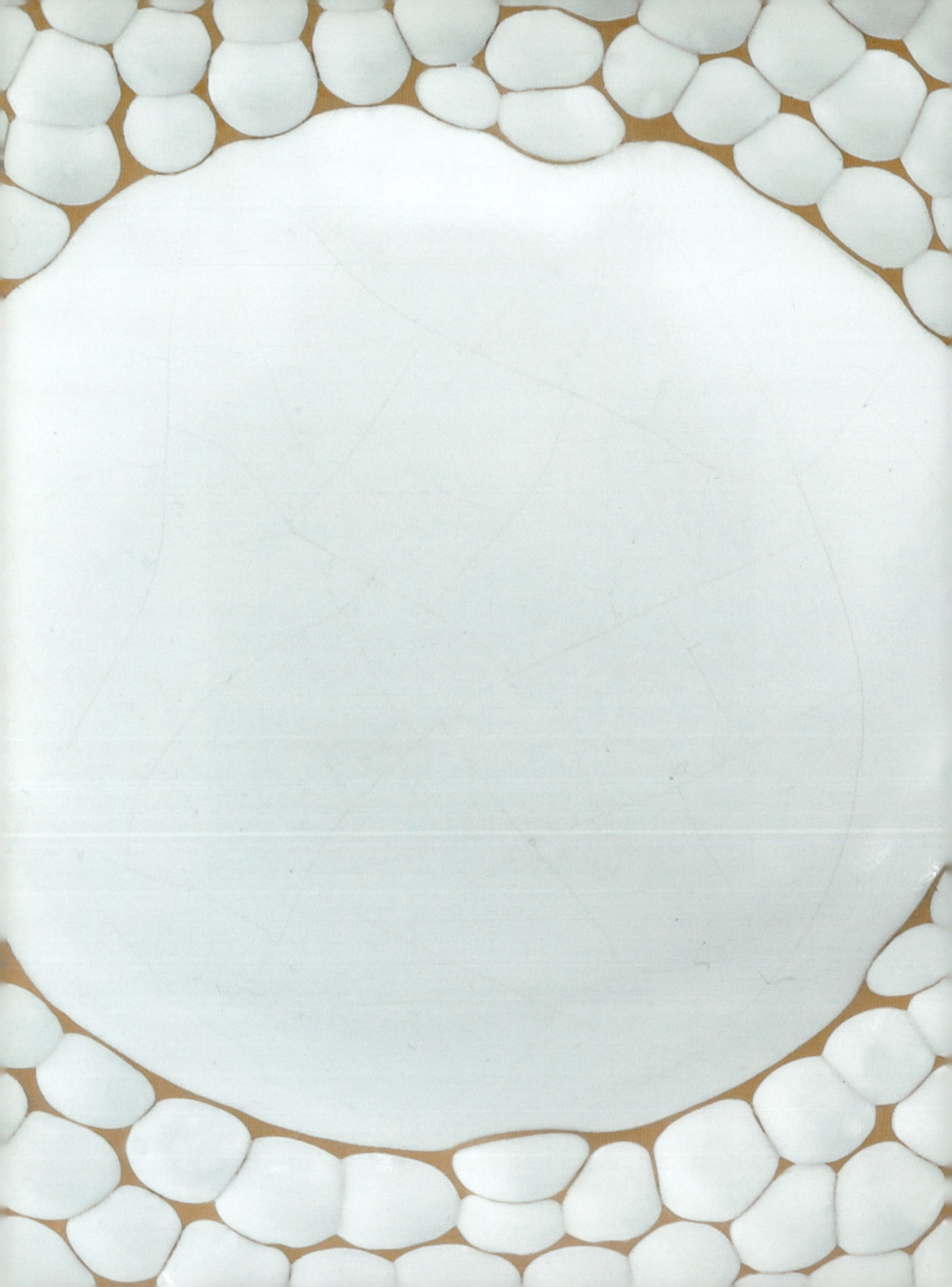

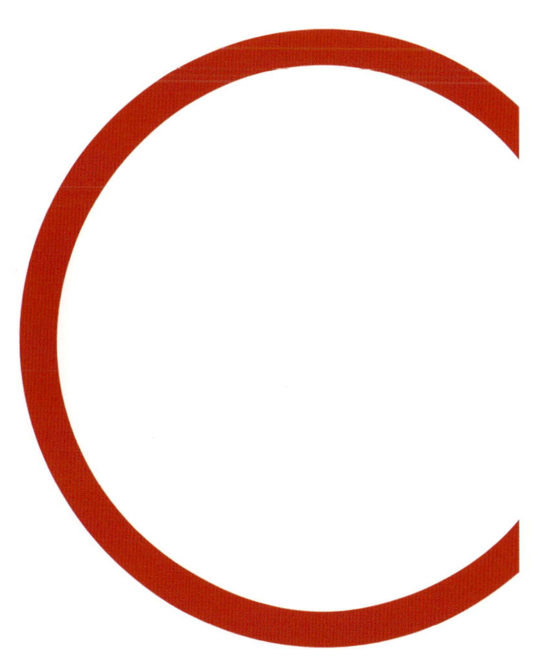

CERAMICS

CERAMICS

The ceramic art in Wilfred Fletcher's current donation to the Boise Art Museum is a smaller component of his overall gift, perhaps reflecting the proportion of the medium's share of his collection generally. Yet, one is struck not only by the quality of the pieces, but by the stature of the artists represented.

Peter Voulkos, who died in 2002, can, without exaggeration, be called the Picasso of ceramic sculpture. The 1950s were a time when ceramists were in transition from simply producing functional pottery to exploring such aesthetic considerations as texture, asymmetrical coiled techniques, combinations of slab and thrown forms, and the use of mixed media. It was a time of shedding the subservient "craft" designation and moving into the realm of fine art, heralding the arrival of ceramic sculpture. Voulkos was perhaps the leading figure in bringing about this change. Innovative and competitive, he began pushing traditional techniques in new directions, and by the mid-to-late 50s had moved on to large clay forms influenced by the abstract expressionists, particularly the work of Franz Kline. In 1954 he founded the art ceramics department at the Los Angeles County Art Institute, where his work became increasingly abstract and sculptural.

Fletcher has donated two small-scale pieces from the 1990s by Voulkos, although the artist was inclined to much larger statements in clay. Nevertheless, despite their size, these at BAM incorporate the characteristics his sculpture is most known for, a visual weight and density, freely formed construction, and an aggressive approach to surface texture. *Untitled Tea Bowl* (1990) and *Untitled Tea Bowl* (1999) are, in other words, miniature versions of his large-scale work, created in stoneware, his favorite medium. They seem to embody both a modernist spirit and a primordial inventiveness.

Jun Kaneko, another transformative force in ceramic art, is in many ways a soul mate of Voulkos, which is not surprising given that he studied with Voulkos and was his studio assistant for a time at the University of California, Berkeley, ceramics department. Born in Japan, where he studied painting, Kaneko came to the U.S. in 1963 to continue his painting studies at the Chouinard Institute in Los Angeles and soon became involved in the ceramic program there. For both Kaneko and Voulkos, the heroics of abstract expressionism in painting signaled an era of endless opportunities that inspired the innovations in their sculptural art.

As Kaneko's exhibition at BAM (November, 2008 to February, 2009) brought home to us, he has remained as much a painter at heart as he has a ceramic sculptor. He is fascinated by the possibilities that the surfaces of his handsomely glazed ceramic pieces present as canvases for manipulating dots, stripes, geometrics and sketches, creating three-dimensional paintings as in his 2009 *Dango*, one of two pieces in this collection. The abstract, organically shaped ceramic sculpture itself seems monumental in scale despite being a mere two feet in height, an illusion perhaps enhanced by its hybrid surface of hard edge forms and Cy Twombly-like freehand drawing. The philosopher/art critic Arthur Danto has written that "Kaneko's most distinctive achievement as a ceramist has been the creation of works that are at once intimate and megalithic…"[1] Both of the Kaneko works donated to BAM underscore this insight.

Another ceramic artist in the collection who has made a career of challenging tradition is Peter Shire. A native of Los Angeles, where he is still based today, Shire has drawn from Bauhaus, Futurist, Art Nouveau and Art Deco precedents but has remained committed to an aesthetic that is free of preconceived norms and ideas. His association with the collective of Italian designers called Memphis has enabled him to experiment in other disciplines, including furniture design. The two works here are beautifully painted ceramic plates, covered in elaborate compositions that mark both his independence and eclectic influences.

Brad Miller's stunning earthenware *Bowl* is finished with a white glazed surface with multiple indentations, to give the piece a unique sense of movement and tension between order and disorder, like a swarm of microscopic life-forms. It is a testimony to Fletcher's eye for the adventurous in this ever-changing art.

---

[1] Arthur Danto, "Dialogues with Clay and Color" (2001) in Susan Peterson, Jun Kaneko (Calmann & King Ltd., London, 2001), 9.

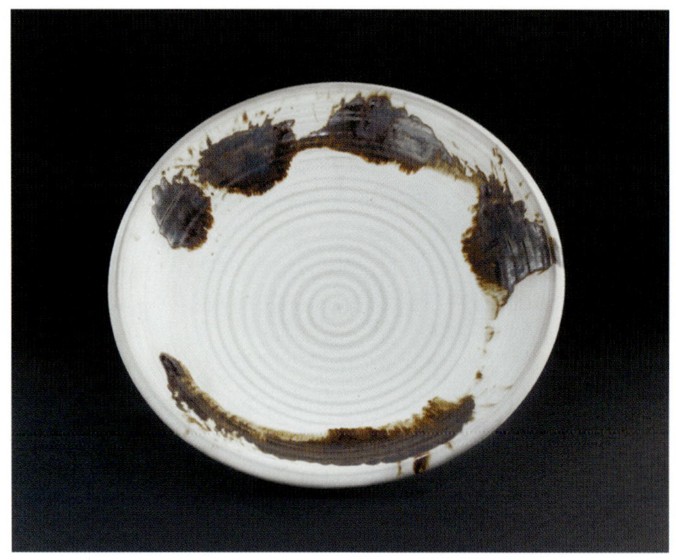

Otto and Vivika Heino | Glaze Fired Bowl | 1995

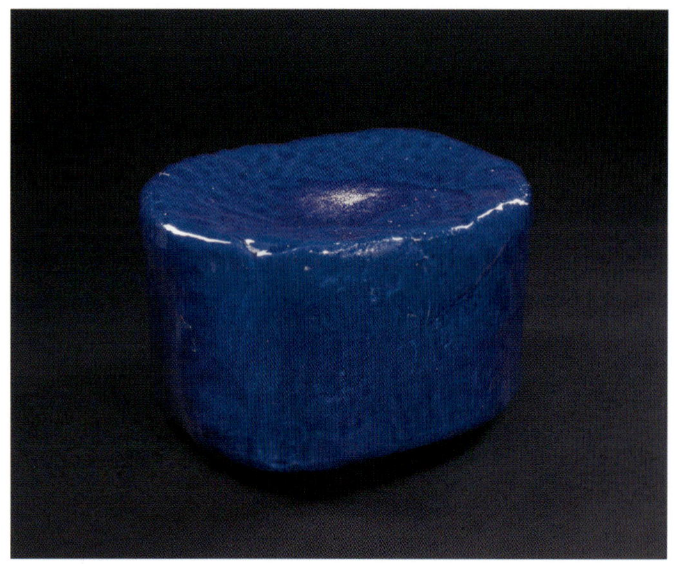

Jun Kaneko | Chunk #91-8-1 | 1991

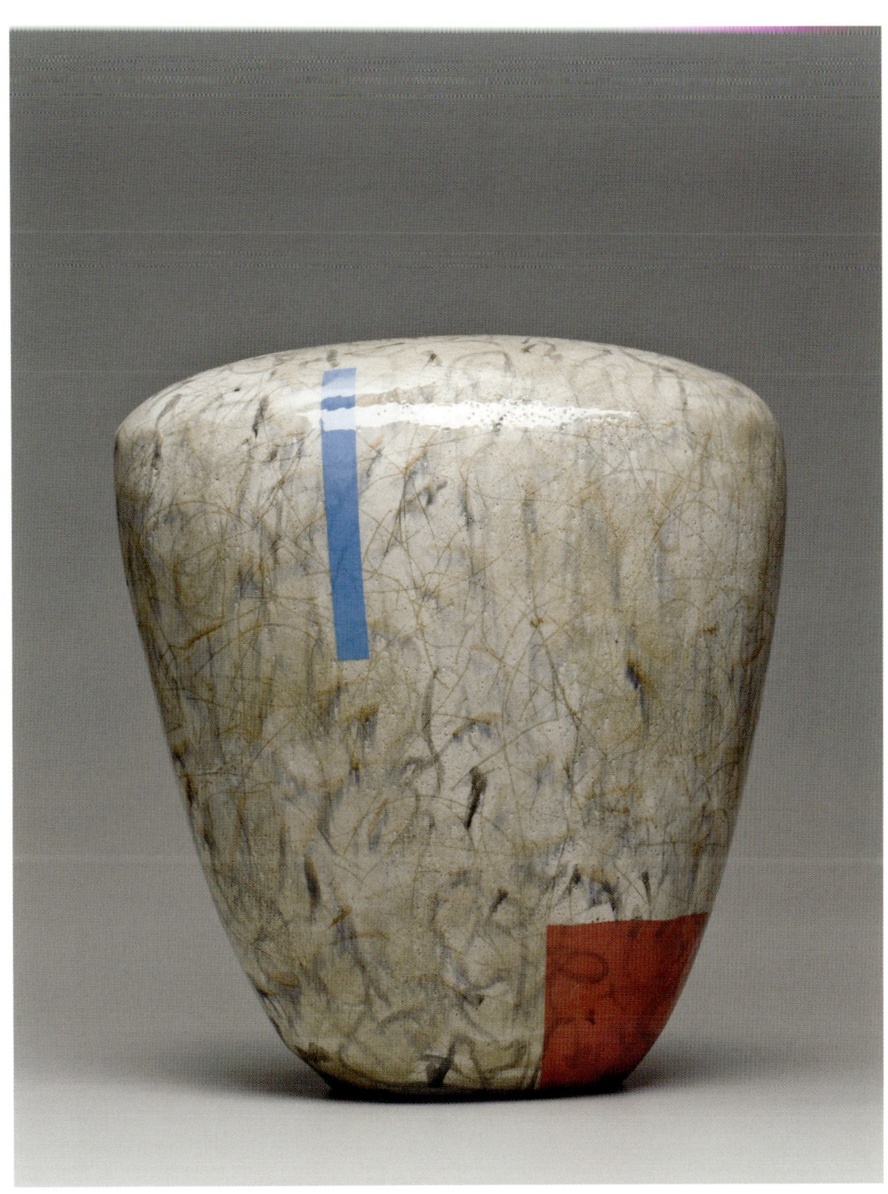

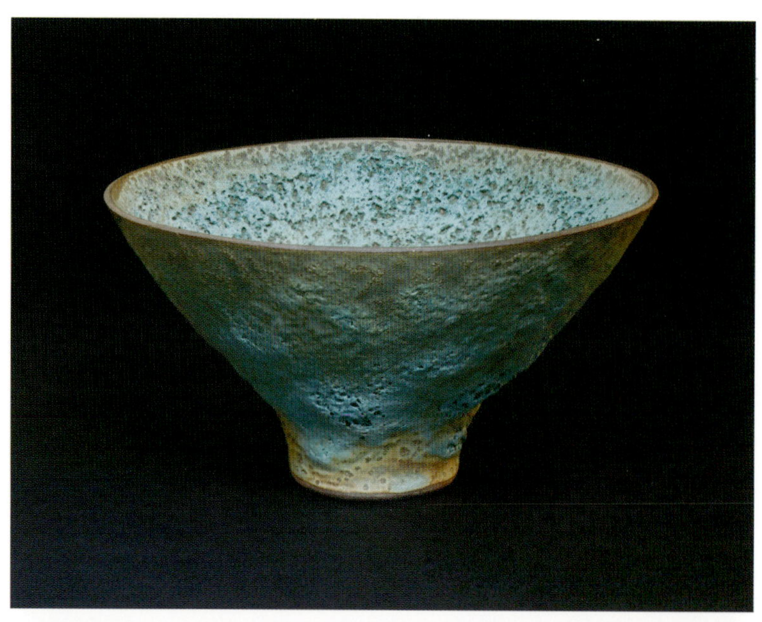

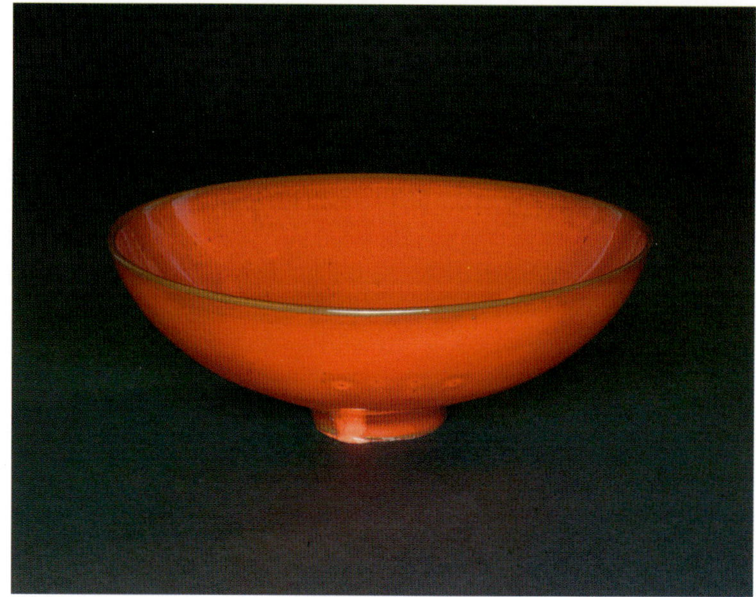

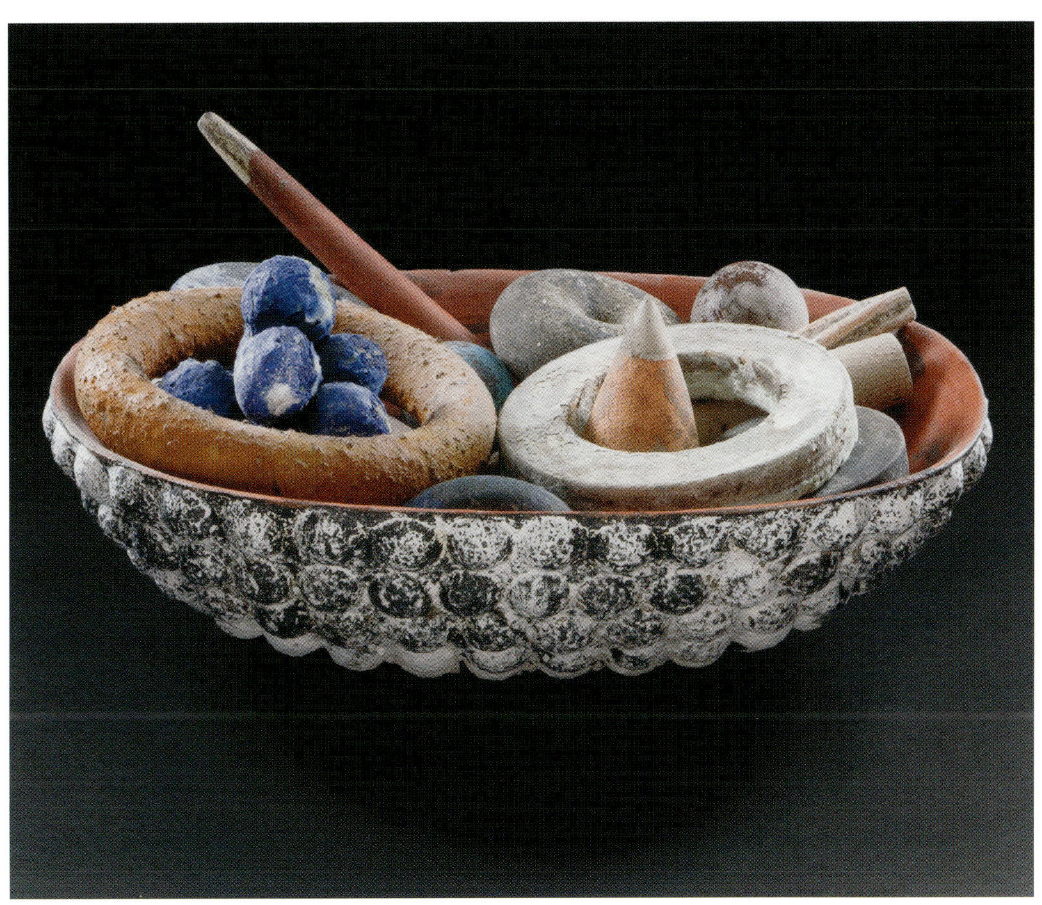

Tony Marsh | Bowl (Radiance and Abundance Series) | 2007

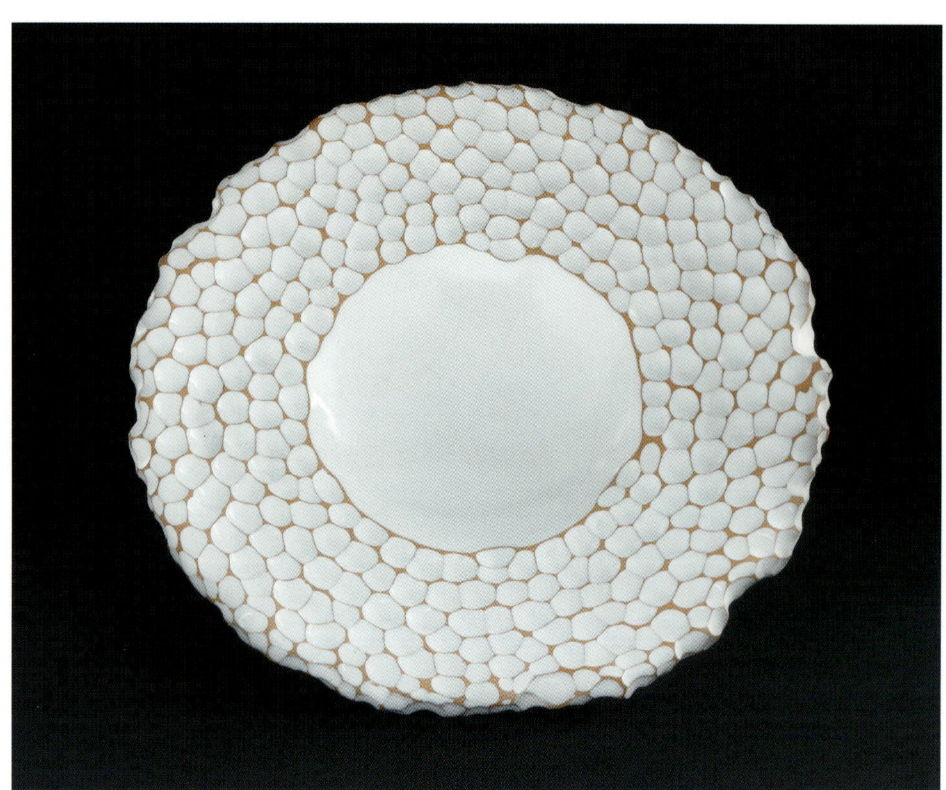

Brad Miller | Bowl | 1997

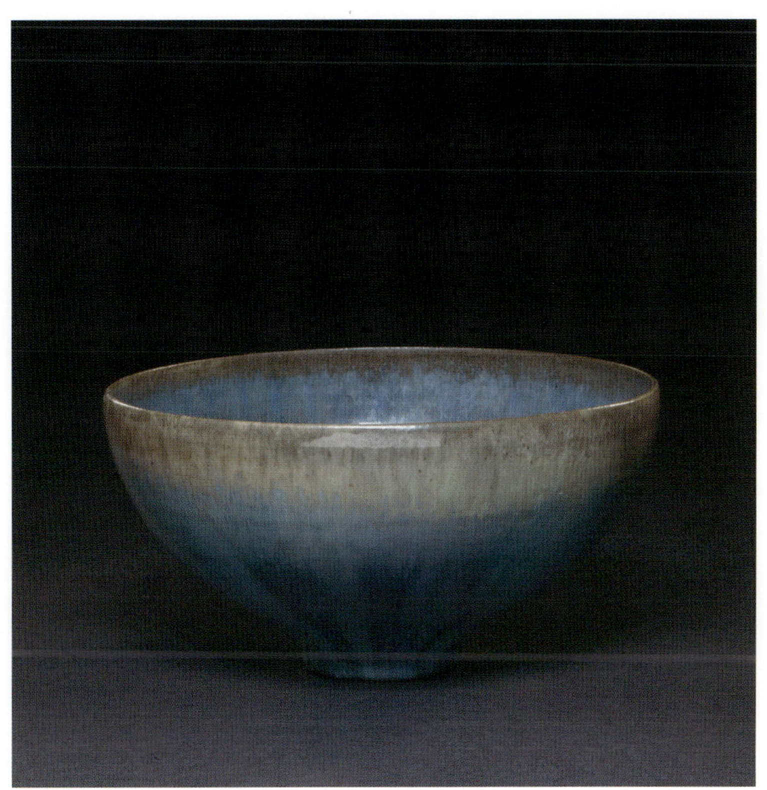

Gertrud and Otto Natzler | Bowl | 1977

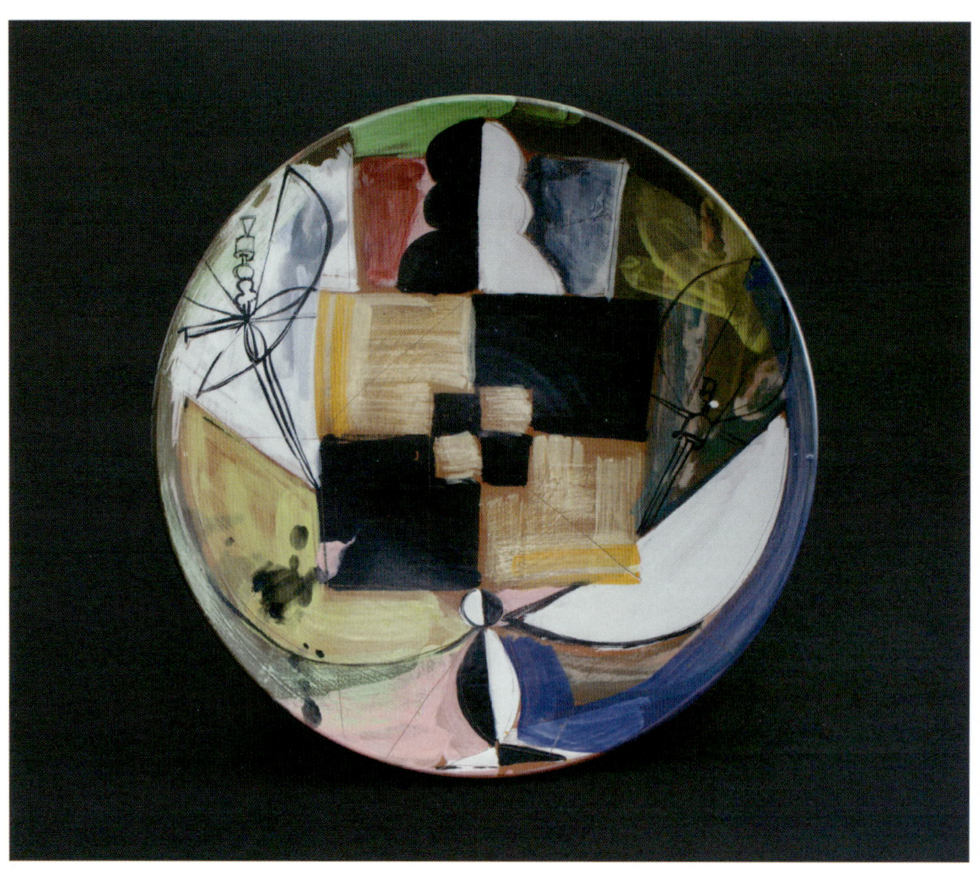

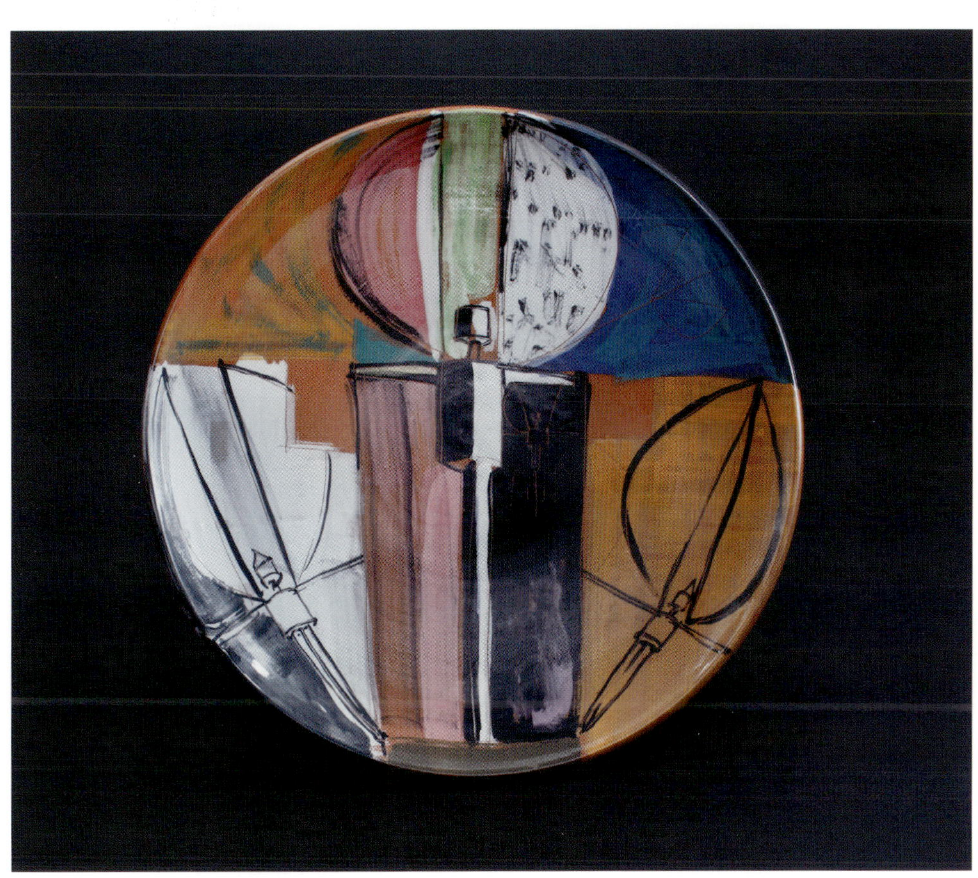

Peter Shire | Set of two Winged Victory Plates | 2000

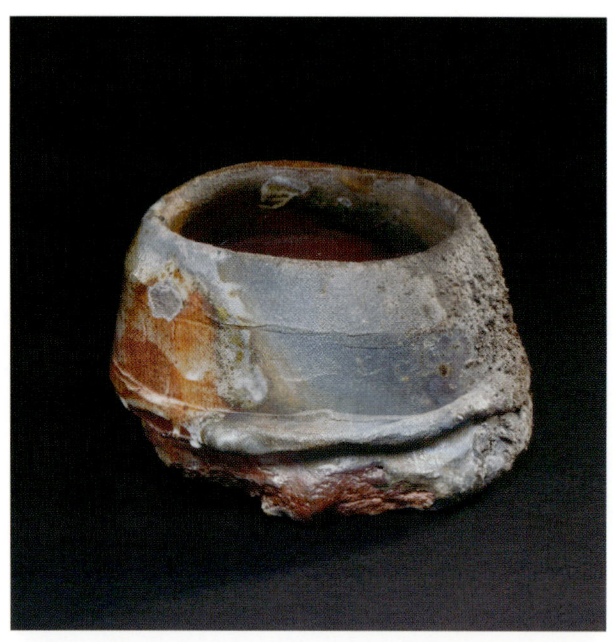

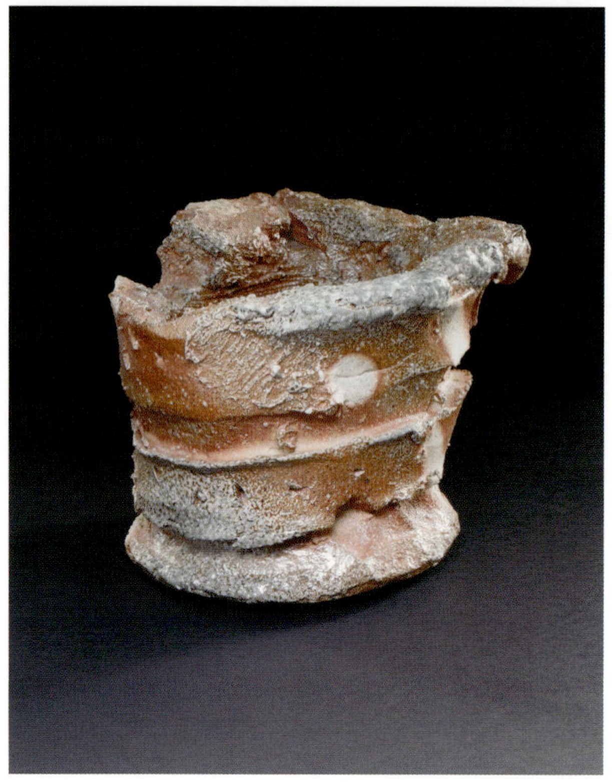

Peter Voulkos | Tea Bowl | 1990 | Tea Bowl | 1999

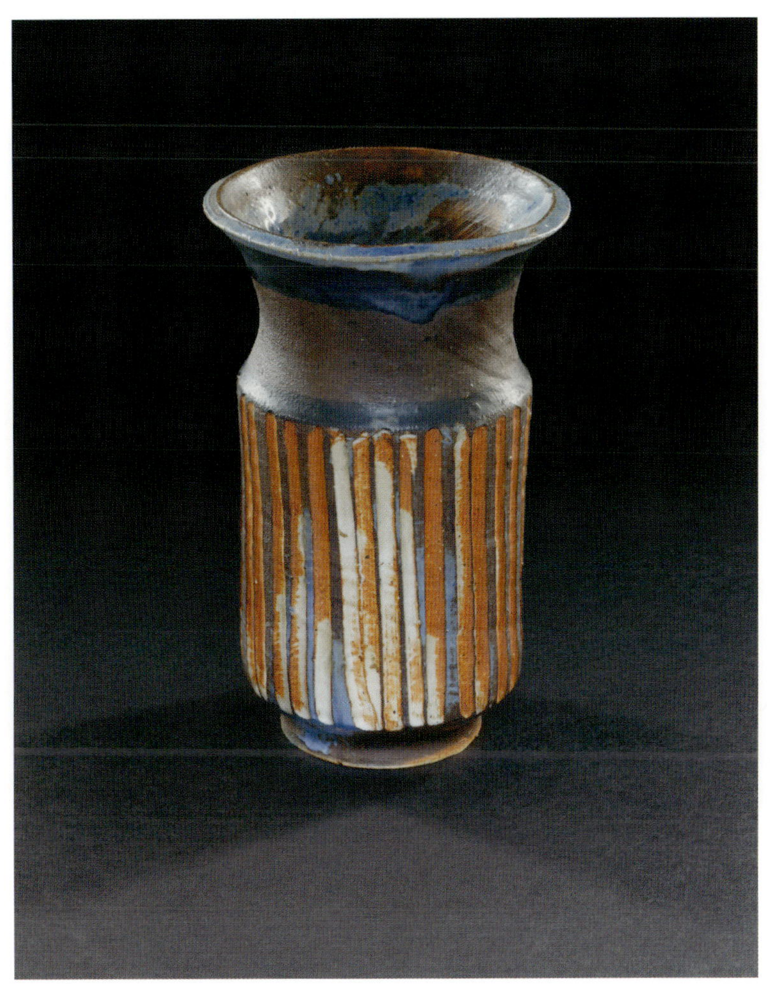

Marguerite Wildenhain | Vessel | circa 1985

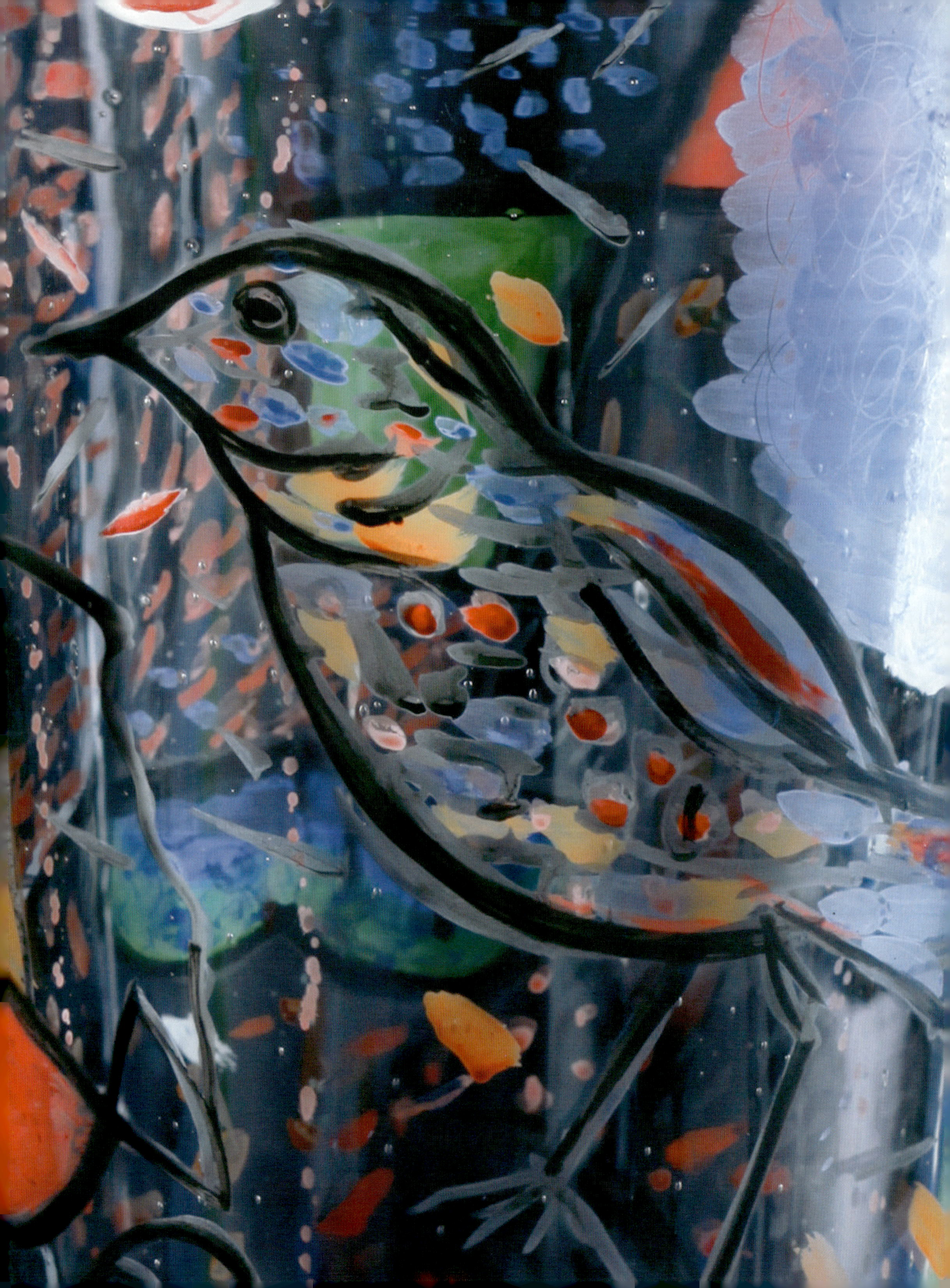

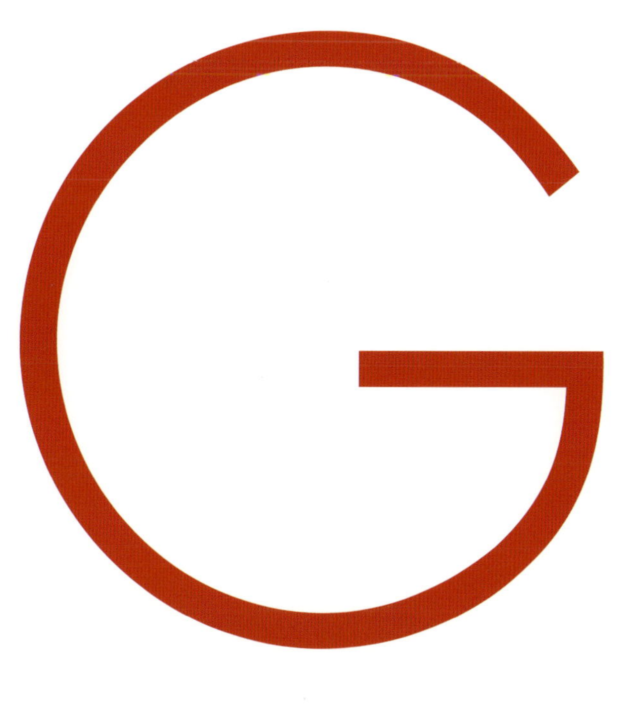

GLASS

It is well known that glassmaking and the use of glass as a decorative medium have been in existence for centuries, but the change in status from an age-old art to a new sculptural art form with aesthetic qualities has, in terms of art history, been fairly recent. Long before Dale Chihuly and his establishment of the Pilchuck Glass School in Stanwood, Washington, came on the scene, 20th-century modernists like Marcel Duchamp were experimenting with glass as an artistic medium. Duchamp's famous *The Bride Stripped Bare by Her Bachelors, Even* (1915-1923), comprised of large panes of clear fractured glass, with mechanical imagery painted in oil and the cobwebs of cracks as part of the design, was the wake-up call that glass and its properties had a role in avant-garde art. Duchamp was fascinated with the medium and discussed it extensively in his writings on art.

As we have seen in the sculpture section of the current Fletcher Collection donation, Claire Falkenstein experimented with combining welded steel and fused, colored glass to create unique, tentacle-like abstract compositions. She was also celebrated for her innovative abstract, stained-glass work in a number of high-profile commissions. The abstract sculptor Italo Scanga worked in hand blown, painted glass, as seen here in his 1987 *Vase*. This art form allowed Scanga to achieve results similar to his multi-sided painted wood sculpture, *Head 78*, which offered several various perspectives to the viewer. His richly painted abstract and figurative imagery encircling *Vase* gave him the opportunity to present the same effect in a totally different medium. In fact, Scanga would be among the first non-glass artists to be invited as an artist-in-residence at Pilchuck.

The glass-art pieces donated by Fletcher to the Boise Art Museum include several notable pioneers both from this country and abroad. The Swedish artist Bertil Vallien (who spent time in Los Angeles) is recognized for developing and perfecting the modern technique of sand-casting glass shapes by creating molds of clean sand mixed with a little water-absorbing clay bentonite, a bonding material. Vallien invented the technique of placing a glass or other object inside the mold during the pouring process to give the appearance of an object floating within the resulting solid glass piece. An example is in this collection, the 1998 *Intersection II*, a cast, egg-shaped head with geometric elements that give it the appearance of an alien mask or helmet, a male figure haunting its interior. Vallien is famous for his sculpted glass masks and heads for which he developed ways to introduce a range of surface markings and effects during the casting process (as is evident here in this piece.) His eerie heads are often displayed on their side like a rare find at an archeological dig.

Seattle artist Sonja Blomdahl learned to make glass art at the Massachusetts College of Art and taught at the Pilchuck Glass School. She also studied with the Venetian master Checco Ongaro, with whom she perfected the process of the double-bubble blowing (incalmo) technique, which is the basis of her reputation. Her hand blown *Blomma Vase* is an example of the beautiful deep colors and refined symmetry characteristic of her work.

Of course, the Pacific Northwest is also where Dale Chihuly, through his work over the decades, has distinguished himself as one of the pre-eminent glass artists of our time. Although a signature extravagance has come to dominate many of his larger projects, it is with his smaller, earlier works by his own hands that we get an idea of his innovations. Fletcher has included *Red Blanket Cylinder*, a semi-opaque orange work that is a painting in the round, with dark decorative lines dominating the top half and dice like motifs and free-drawn lines below. Its geometry and freehand painterly additions make us forget it is based on a traditional craft that originally signified a utilitarian purpose and see it as a consummate piece of abstract art that echoes Native American design, Art Deco, and minimalism.

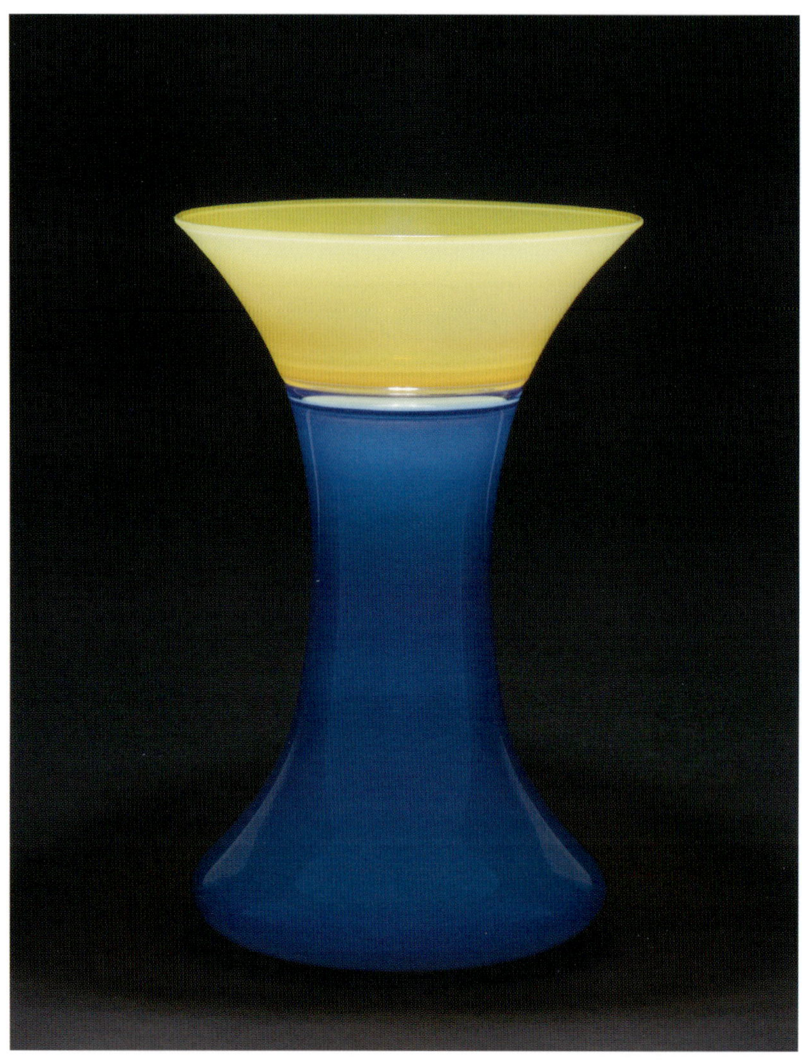

Sonja Blomdahl | Blomma Vase | 2004

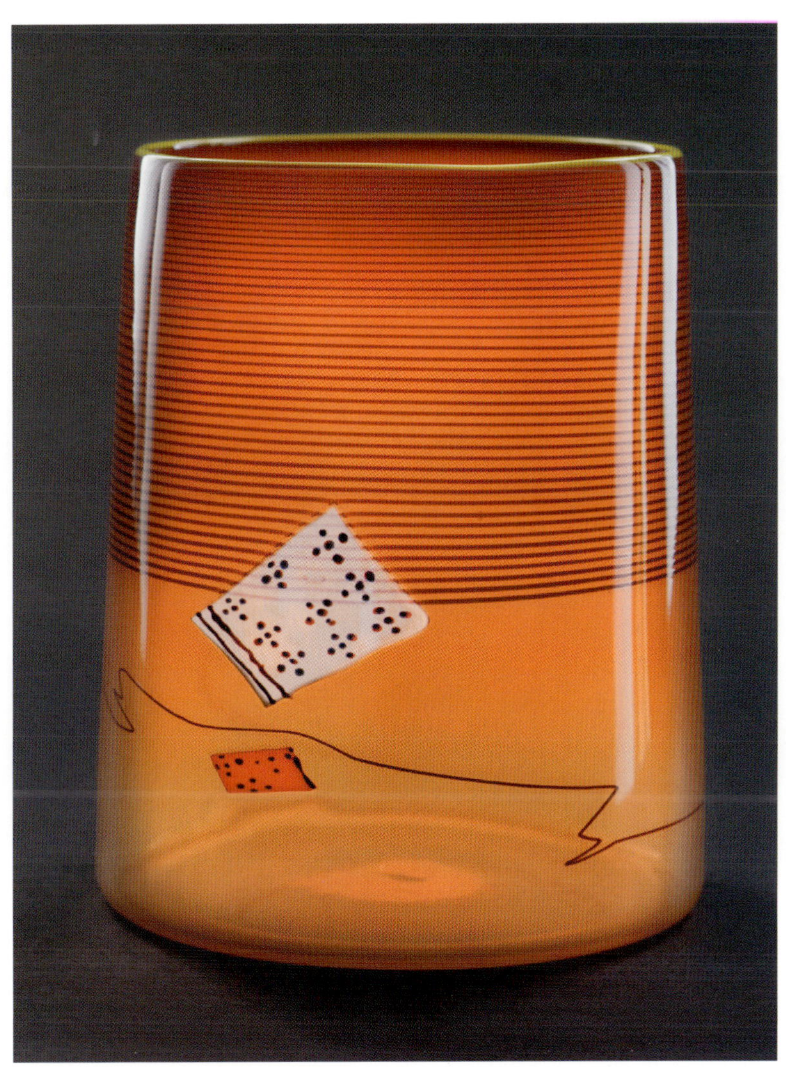

Dale Chihuly | Red Blanket Cylinder | 2000

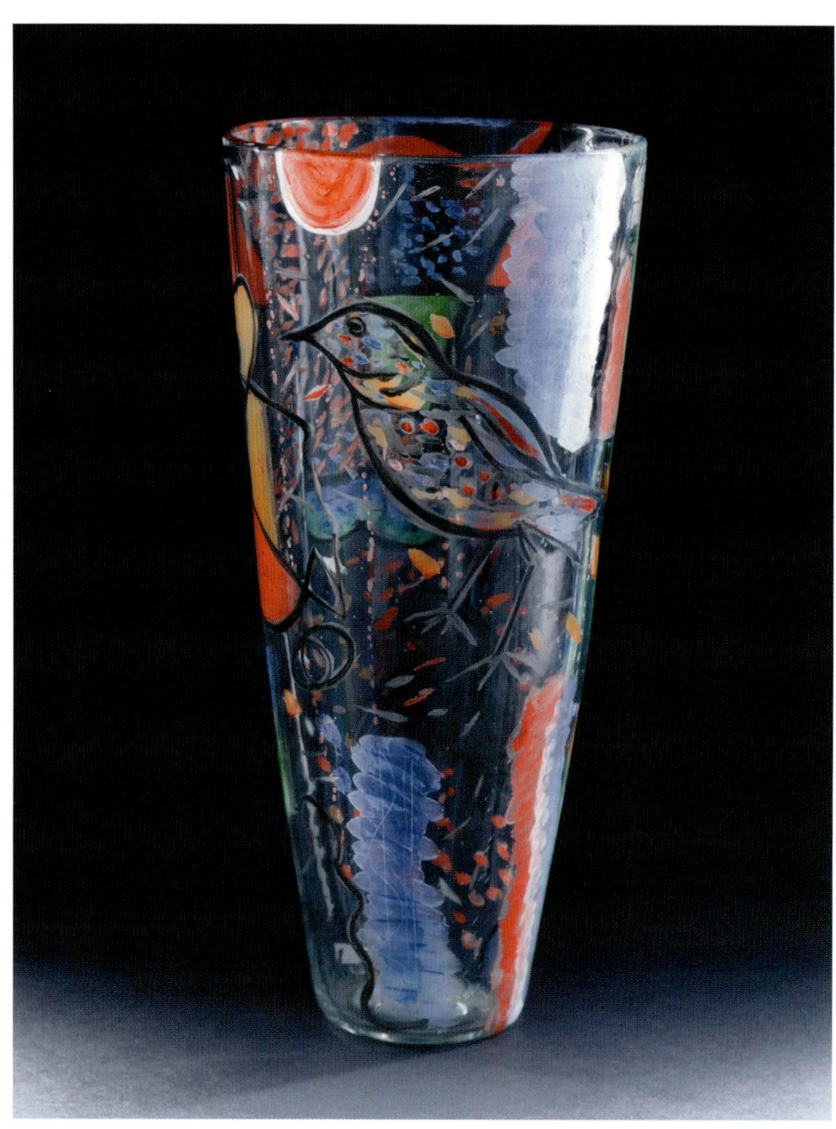

Italo Scanga | Vase | 1987

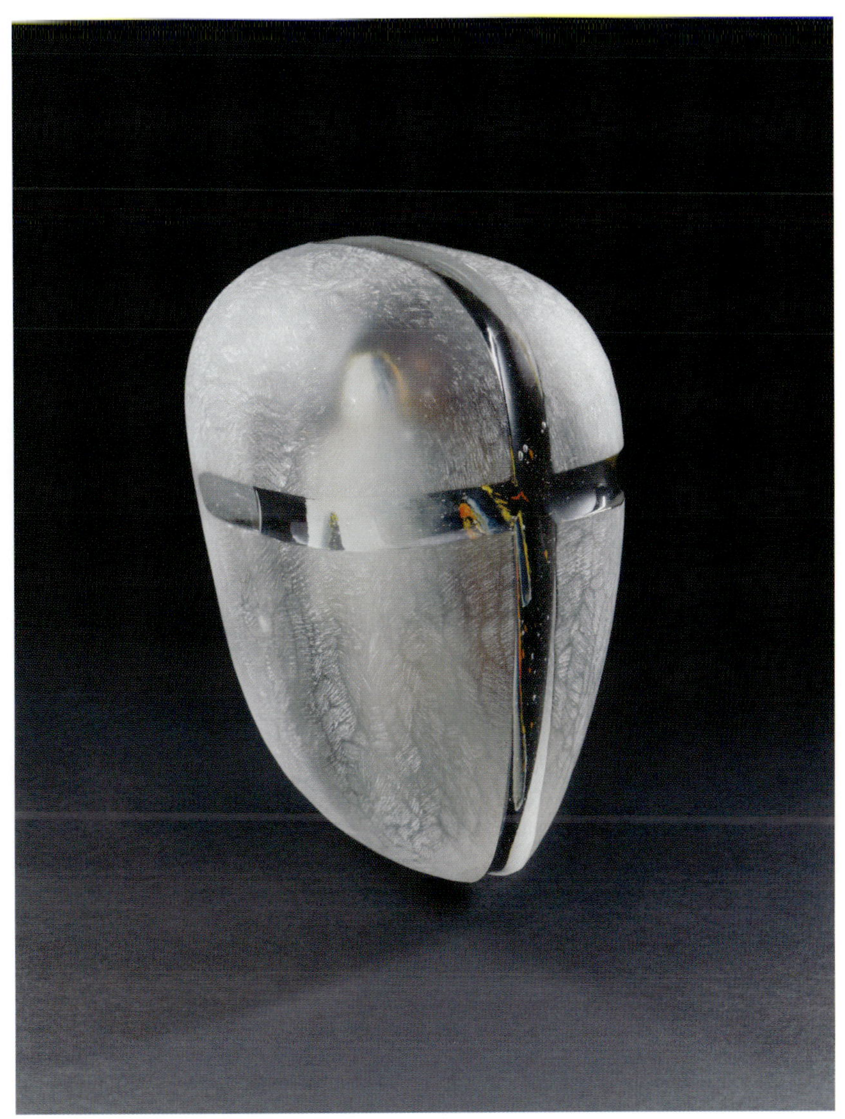

Bertil Vallien | Intersection II | 1998

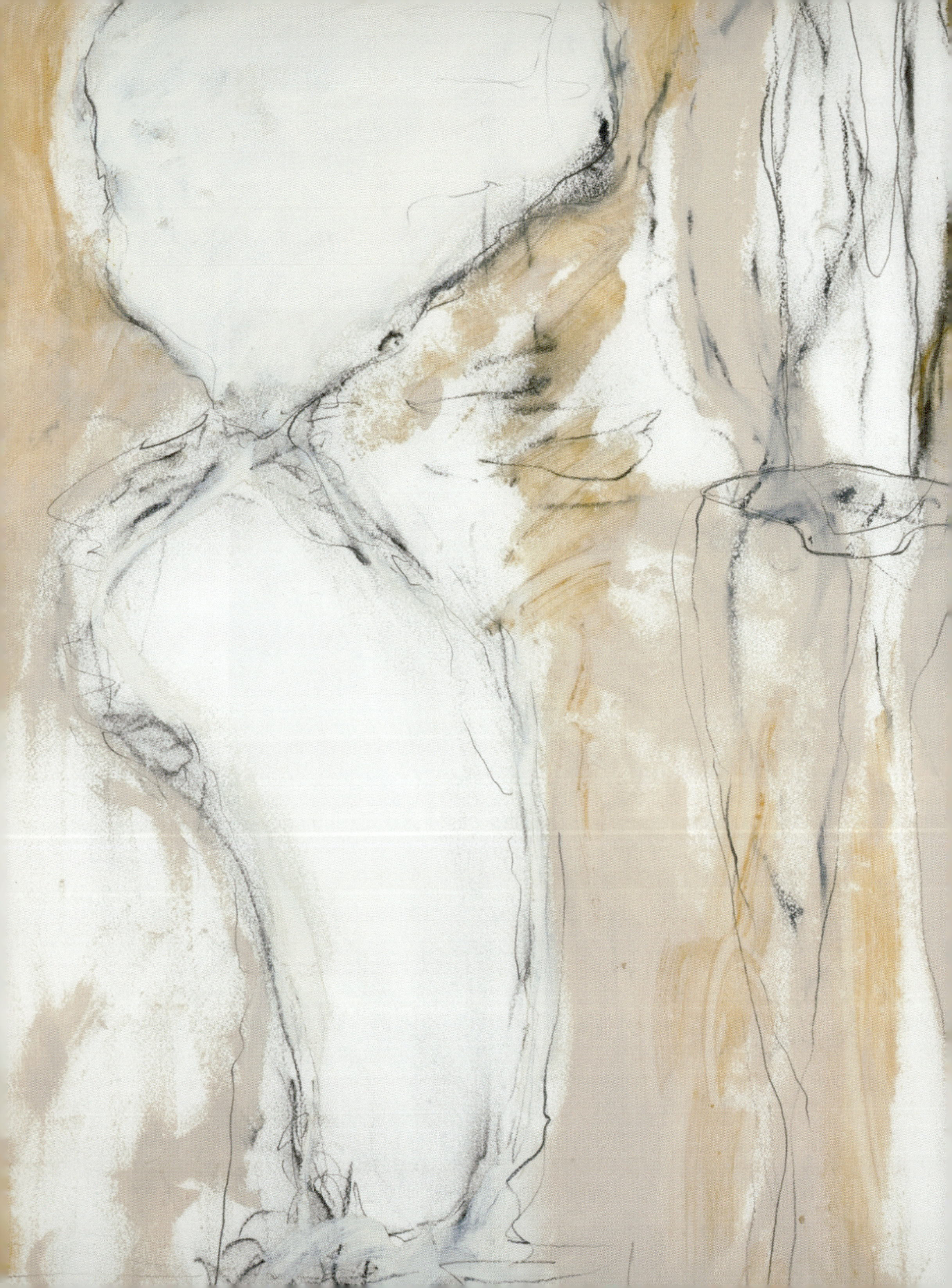

P

WORKS ON PAPER

The designation "works on paper" refers to individual images which, basically, are paintings done in a variety of mediums, usually water-based like watercolors and gouache, but also acrylic, which lend themselves to creating a singular effect via their interaction with the paper's surface and its absorbent qualities. This genre is also friendly to mixed media techniques and experimentation in general.

The Fletcher Collection has impressive holdings in this art form, which, considered with the quality of the prints he has chosen, speaks of an art connoisseur enamored of artwork on fine paper.

Not surprisingly, a few of Fletcher's favorite artists are represented in this section as well. Charles Arnoldi, the sculptor, once again displays his interest in the two-dimensional. *Untitled* (1999) is a gouache on a ground of collaged rectangular-shaped paper. It is a painted composition comprised of soft, floating abstract forms, not unlike those in a lava lamp, which migrate across the multi-colored, rectilinear background. The result is another unexpected divergence from his sculptural work. Sam Francis makes an appearance here, too, with his untitled acrylic on paper from 1989, which again demonstrates his debt to Jackson Pollock in technique and consideration of space while relying on his own brazen palette.

The works on paper in Fletcher's collection do us the favor of bringing back to our attention artists long on the scene but who may have been out of the public eye of late. Ron Davis, who attended the San Francisco Art Institute from 1960 to 1964, would have a significant impact on contemporary abstract painting in the mid-1960s, his *Dodecagon Series* of 1968-69 being particularly influential. Abstract expressionism influenced him, but he was very innovative in the studio, creating geometric shaped, illusionistic paintings with polyester resins and fiberglass. The critics called him inspired, and from early on he was represented by prominent New York and Los Angeles galleries. Davis' art contributed to the hard-edge, shaped-canvas, and color-field movements, and he was involved in the California hi-tech art scene. His large, subdued watercolor on paper here entitled *Three Squares* (*Flatland Series*, 1980) contains three gray- and earth-tone squares made of combined geometric shapes tumbling across the paper like a roll of the dice. It is good to see his special treatment of space, scale and color relationships again.

Joe Goode is another figure from the recent past who pops up here. Born in Oklahoma, he moved to Los Angeles in the late 50s and attended the Chouinard Art Institute. His paintings were initially associated with the Pop Art movement and he was included in the first museum Pop Art exhibition in the U.S. with Lichtenstein, Warhol, Dine, Ruscha and other like-minded luminaries. As his career evolved, Goode took to combining various traditional and non-traditional media in his art, creating images that explored concepts of transparency and manipulation of perspectives in a variety of subjects, from milk bottles to cloud-scattered skies. His striking medium-scale mixed media on collaged photographs called *Fire and Ice* is a startling composition of photos of flames, snow-covered tree branches, and gestural abstract painting of gold, red and white. This work from 2006 shows he still has his flair for drama.

Eric Fischl first made his name in the late 1970s and 1980s, concurrently with the rise of Neo-Expressionism in painting but from which he remained somewhat apart. His dramatically-lit figurative canvases dealt mostly with what Fischl describes as suburban subject matter, which may sound uninteresting but always has an edge to it in his hands. In fact, he has acquired a reputation as the bad boy of art in his depictions of the dark side of the suburban, country-club culture of which he is a product. Adolescent sexuality and voyeurism, women in provocative poses in front of male youths, couples relaxing in the looser sexual mores of the time, have been controversial elements of his observations on the baser instincts underlying a seemingly straight, upper-middle-class social structure. Fischl's *Study for Painting*, a 1995 watercolor on paper, depicts a back view of a nude female with tan marks that show she has been sunbathing topless. Rendered in a casual manner, the nonchalant demeanor of this woman in the buff is characteristic of Fischl's observations on a particular contemporary American lifestyle.

Los Angeles-based artist Ed Moses is a long-term denizen of the California art scene whose art has undergone many changes over his career. After a period of architecture-inspired imagery, Moses shifted to an abstract art in which the layering of surfaces and the role of process in a non-objective aesthetic became overriding concerns that he returned to time and again. The works by Moses in this Fletcher gift capture two distinct periods in his art. In 1971, a more spiritual ambiance entered his work. The evocative, untitled acrylic on laminated tissue paper from 1973 that Fletcher acquired is a fine, transitional piece, a retreat from his more complicated abstractions. The immediacy and delicacy of this large-scale work, with its pale, colored diagonals, has a beckoning, if fleeting, presence. By the late 1990s, Moses was using different materials and tools to create more inventive effects in paint. His *Lar-e-et #4* from 1998, an acrylic painting on mylar, has the feel of controlled chaos, a mosaic in the midst of structural decay. Moses' experimental streak has never waned.

Fletcher's appreciation for Peter Millett's talent in both painting and sculpture led to his acquisition of Millett's 2003 *Blue Rhumba*. This acrylic on paper collage is a handsomely executed piece that simultaneously revisits Millett's early years as a painter and incorporates the formal language of his sculptural work. Its complicated, geometric design of broad planes is dominated by the off-kilter center blue panel that not only challenges the flatness of its surrounding abstract environment but instills a sense of rhythmic energy and three-dimensional depth that is Millett's forte.

This collector's eye for two-dimensional art by sculptural artists rewards us with a rare pastel on paper by the New York-based metal sculptor Joel Shapiro. Shapiro is renowned for his dynamic work in bronze and other metals, composed of geometric shapes that seem to defy gravity, thereby instilling a certain psychology to his art. Shapiro's approach to scale is informed by his belief that small objects can still be monumental, which would resonate with Fletcher as we have seen in the sculpture he collected. The pastel in question here is a study for *Boat, Bird, Mother and Child*, 2008, a deceivingly simple design in black, yellow and red. Its odd geometry reveals Shapiro's attraction to forms not limited or grounded by architectonics or right angles.

Of the many fine works in this category, one of the most dramatic is Pat Steir's large, vertical painting on paper, *Waterfall #23*. Steir brings to her abstractions a blend of Eastern (especially Chinese) aesthetics and culture, abstract expressionist technique, an Agnes Martin-like mystical minimalism, and a knack for bringing conceptual art's emphasis on ideas to life in a poetic way. This piece is part of her ongoing waterfall series, but it is different from her more familiar works in this vein. Taoism's reverence for the four basic elements—earth, air, fire and water—have long influenced her painting, but it has been the properties of water in nature that have been Steir's central metaphor and conceptual vehicle. Here, the brilliant orange-red background and the green at the painting's core bring the elements of fire and earth, respectively, into the picture on an equal footing with water. In this sense, *Waterfall #23* is an all-encompassing meditation on nature, exemplifying the appeal of art on paper.

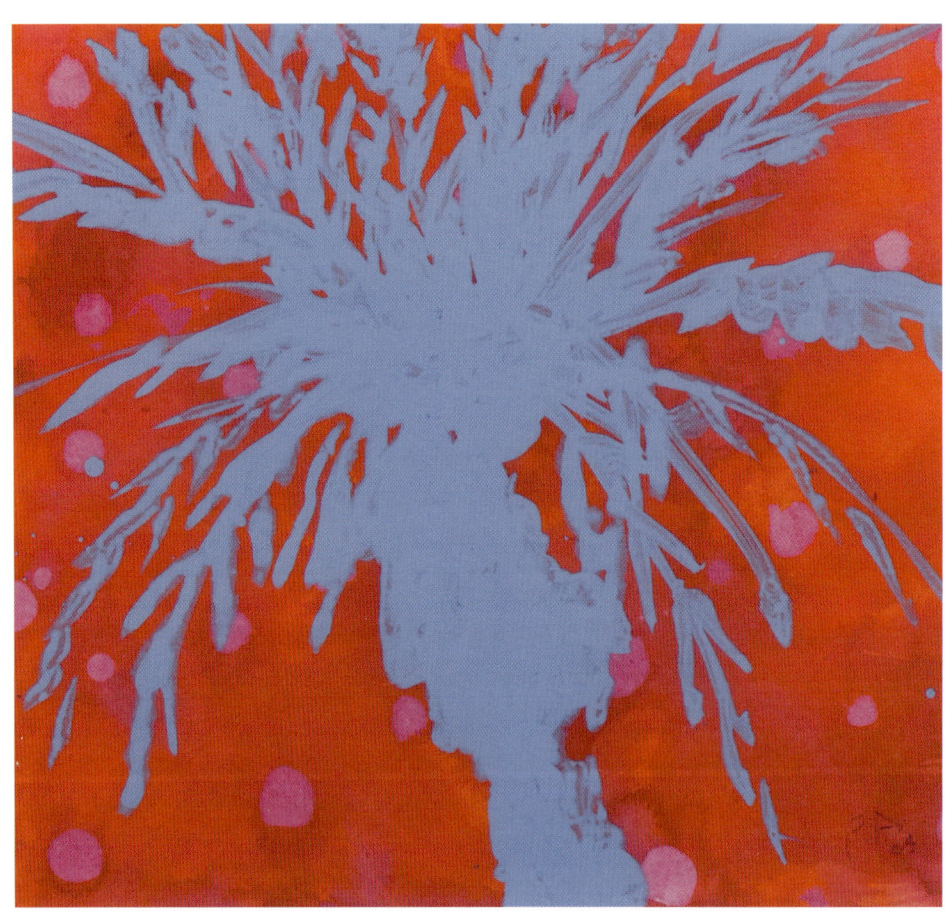

Peter Alexander | Ylang Ylang | 2004

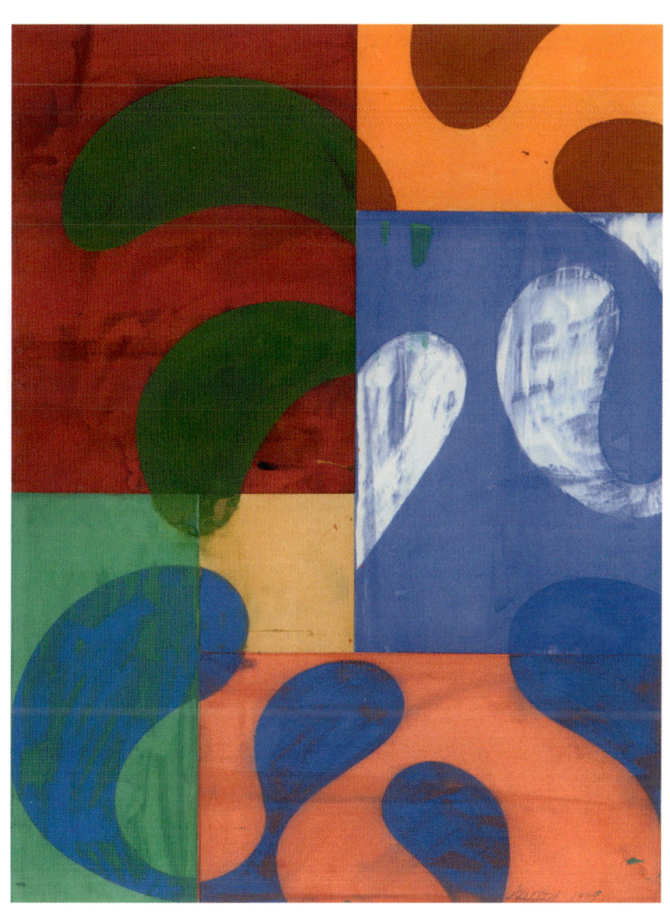

Charles Arnoldi | Untitled | 1999

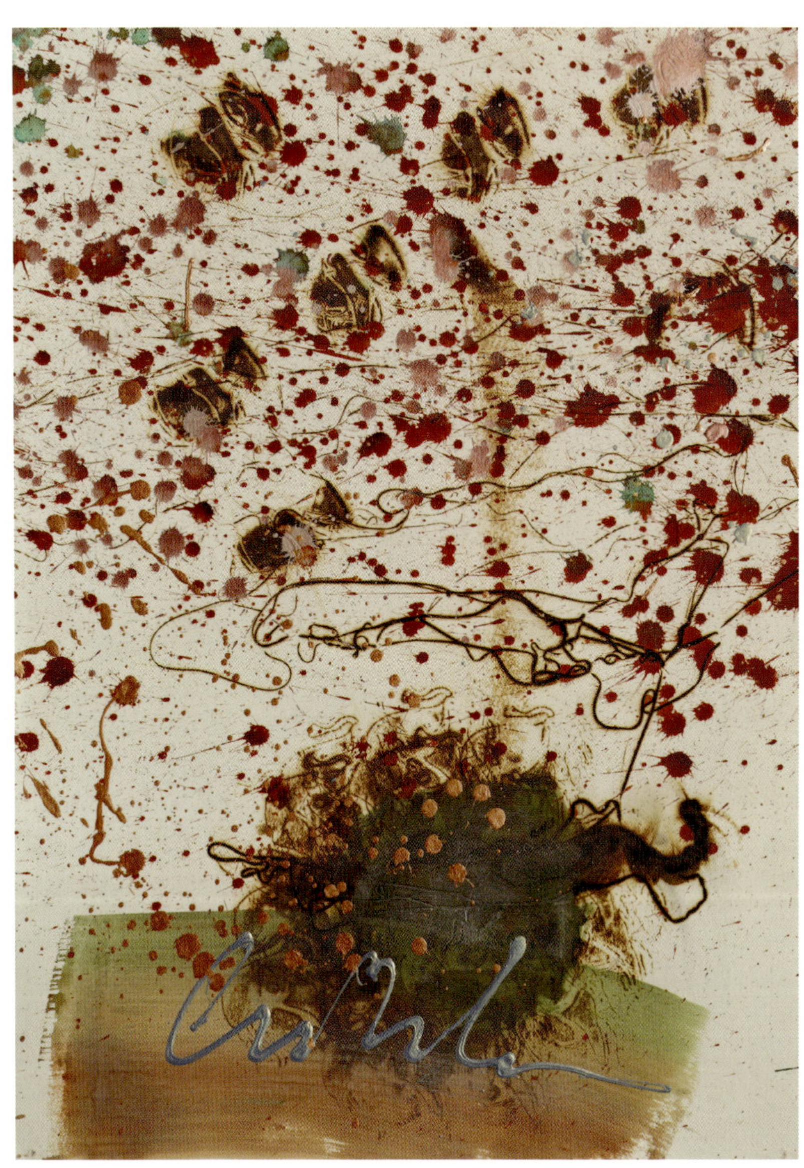

Dale Chihuly | Glass Painting | 2001

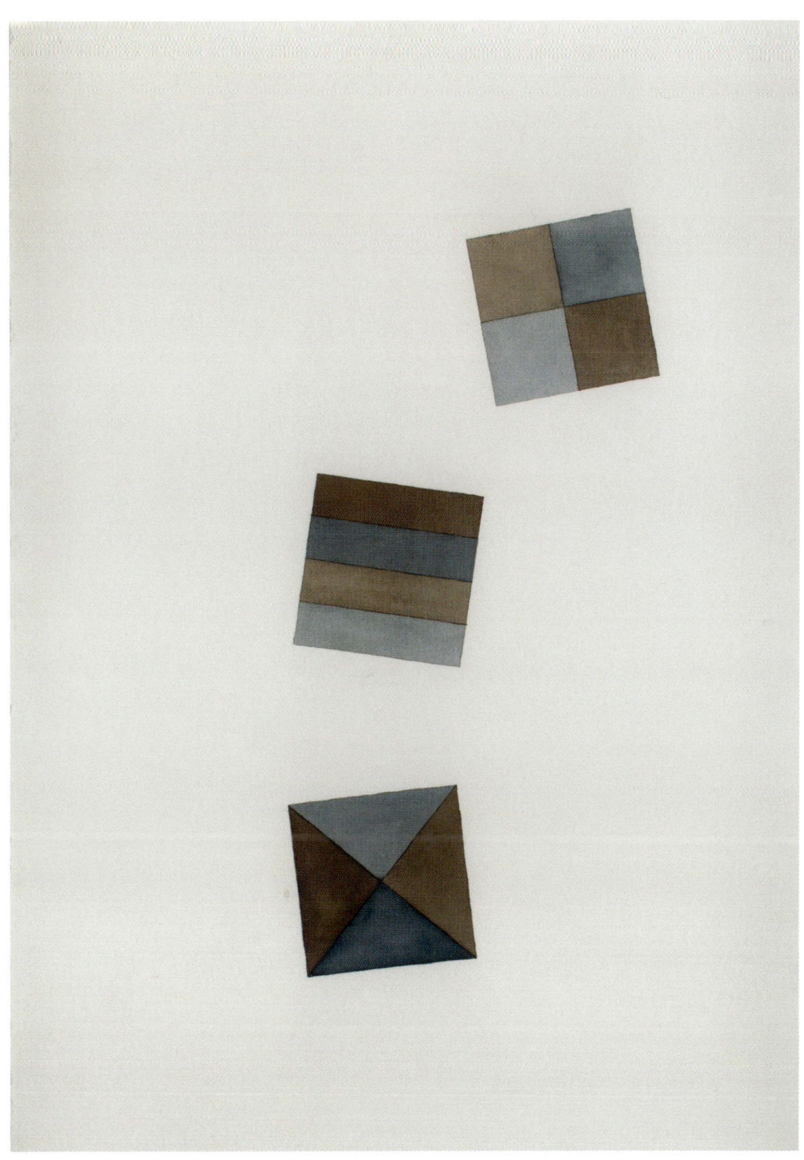

Ronald Davis | Three Squares (Flatland Series) | 1980

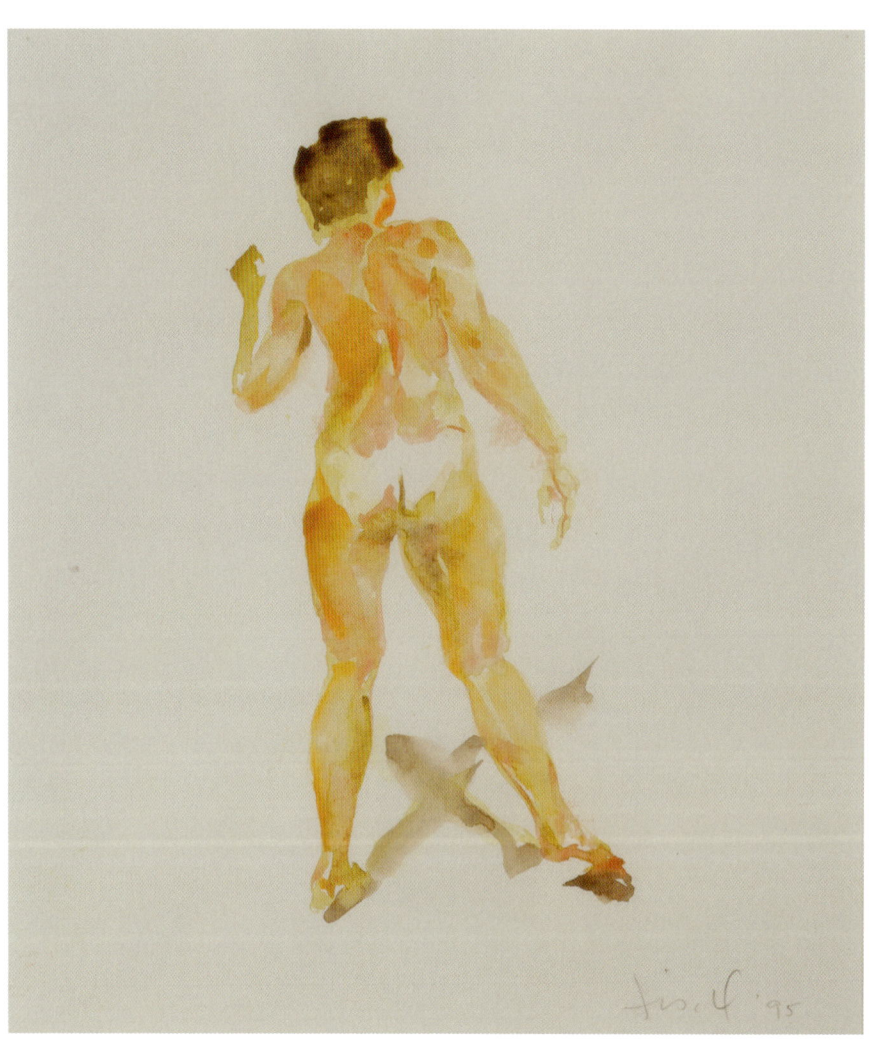

Eric Fischl | Study for Painting | 1995

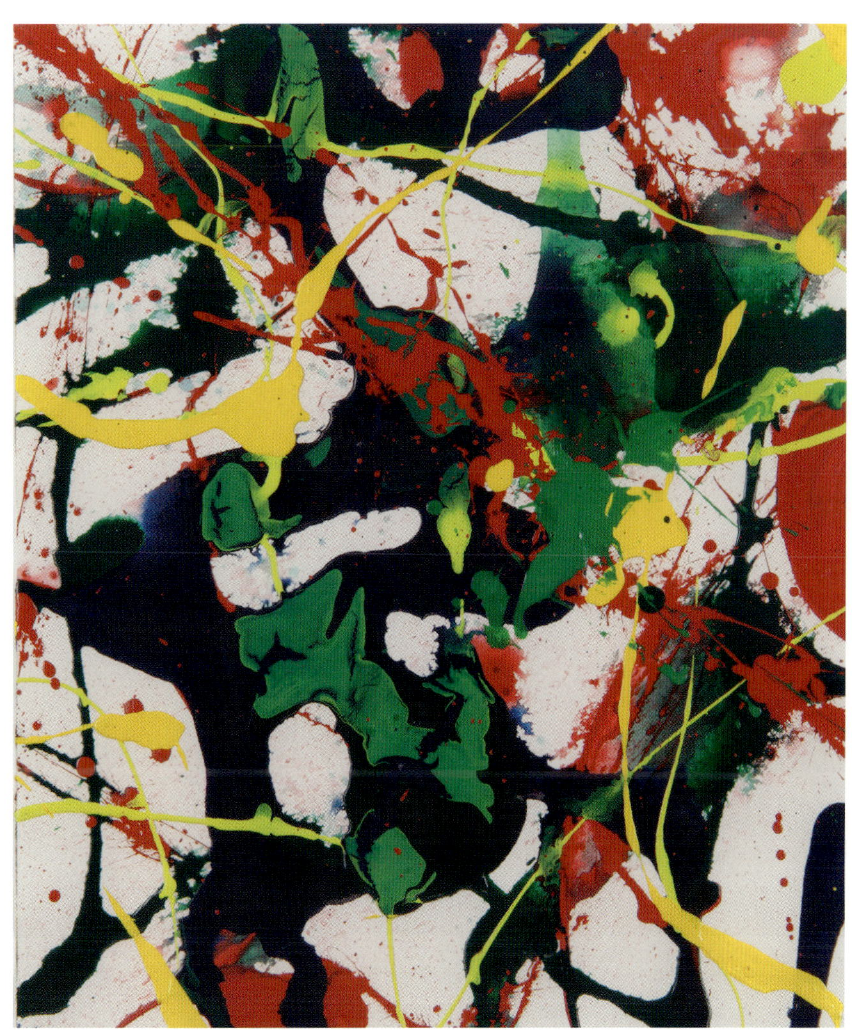

Sam Francis | Untitled | 1989

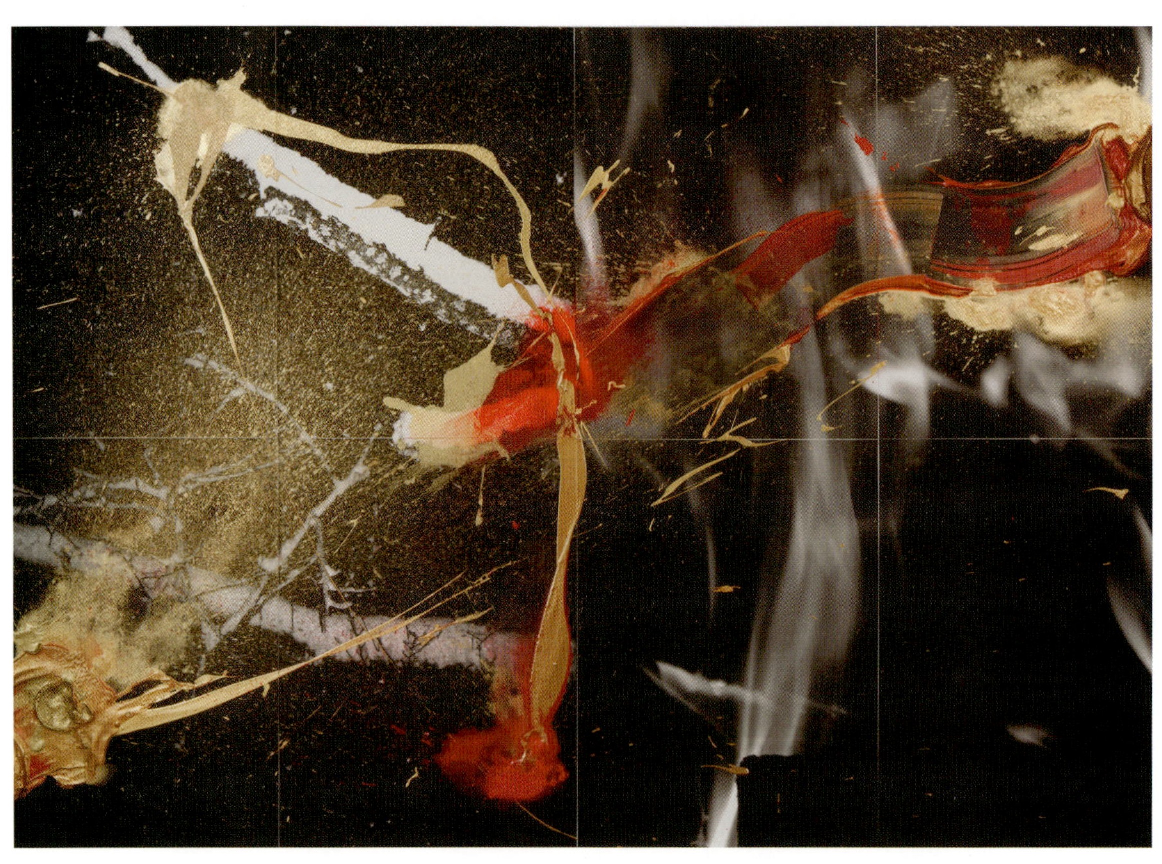

Joe Goode | Fire and Ice | 2006

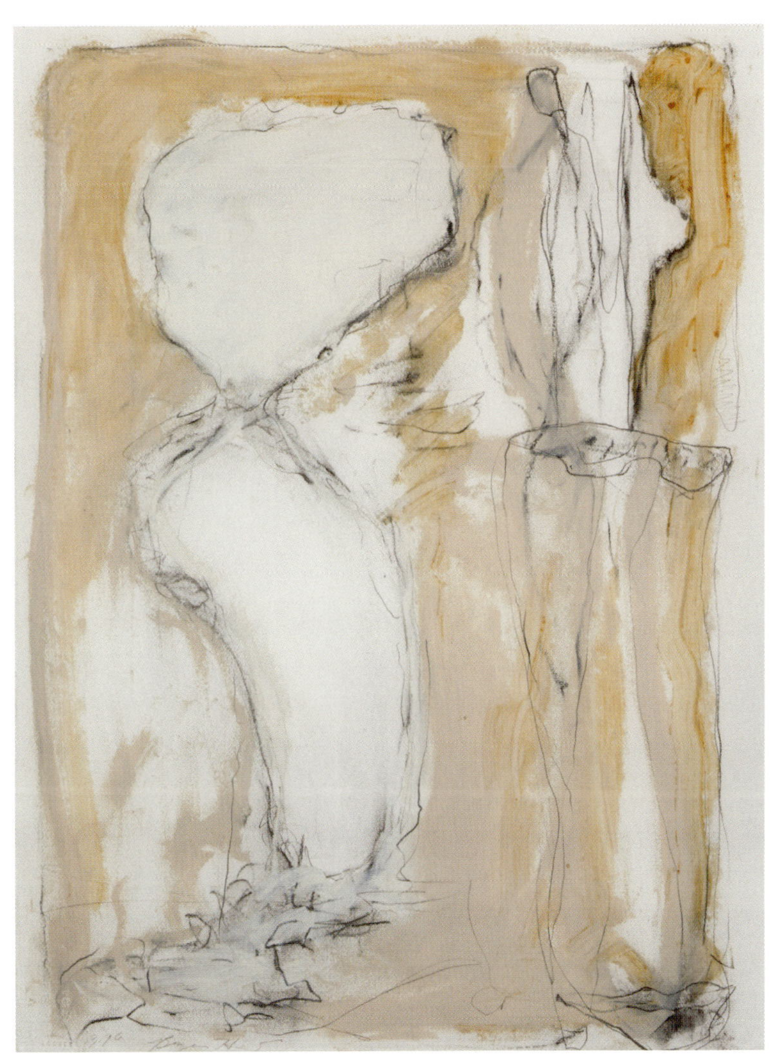

Bryan Hunt | Untitled | 1996

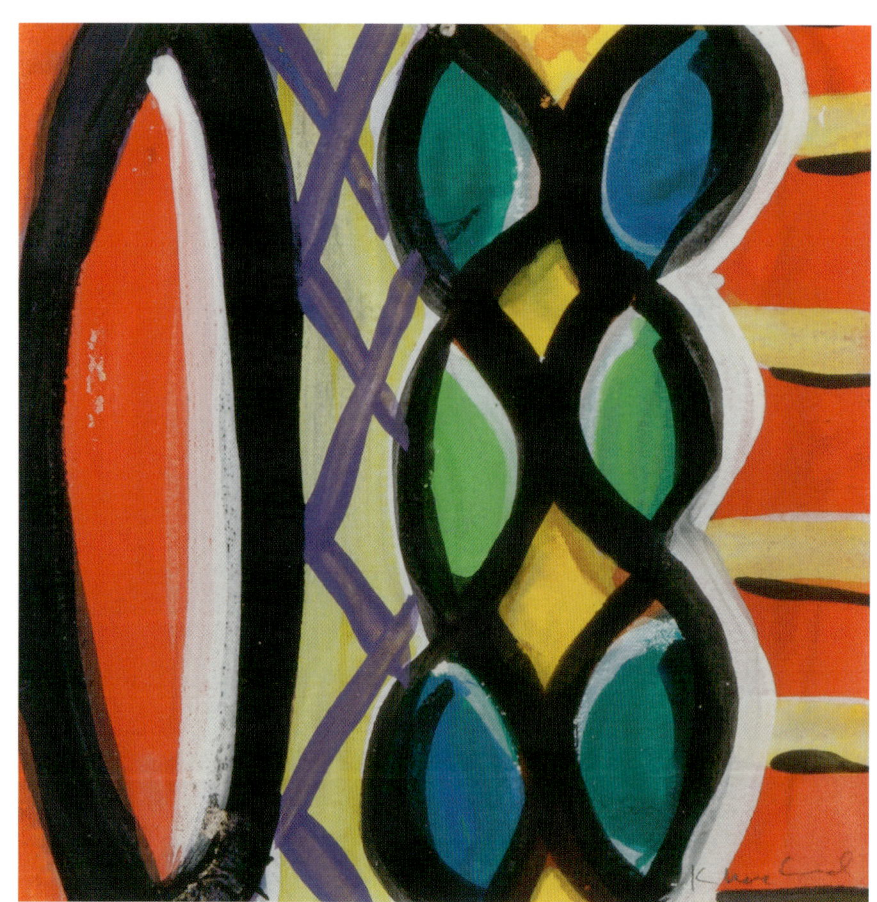

Kim MacConnel | *Woman with Mirror, Gouache #5* | 2007

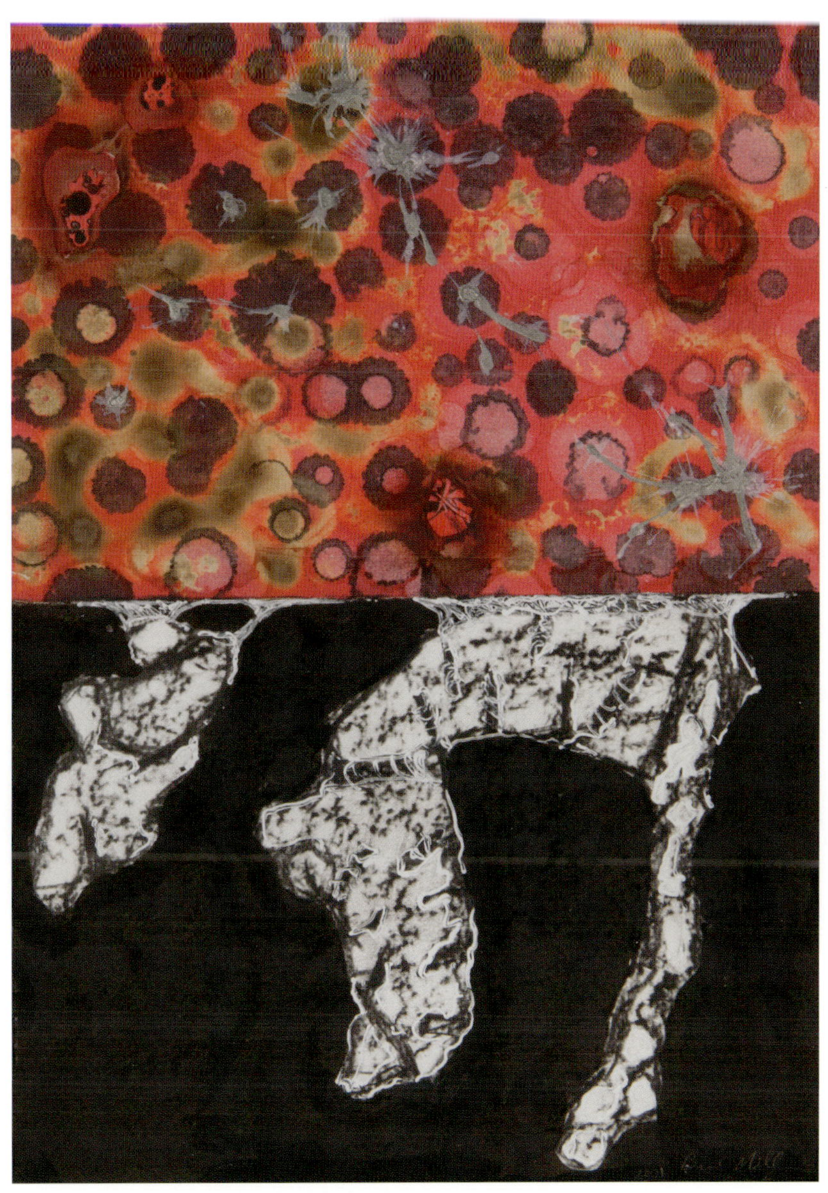

Brad Miller | Untitled | 2001

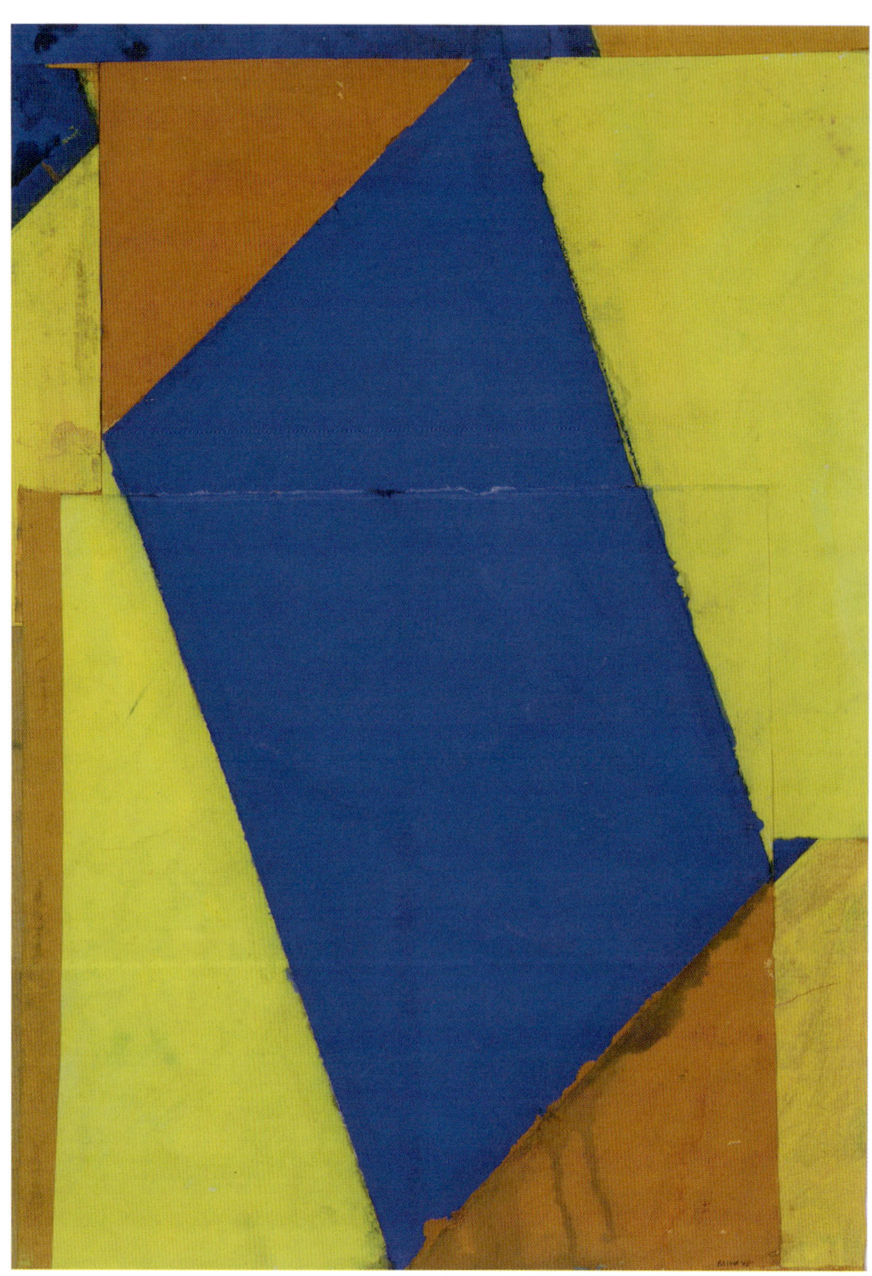

Peter Millett | Blue Rhumba | 2002

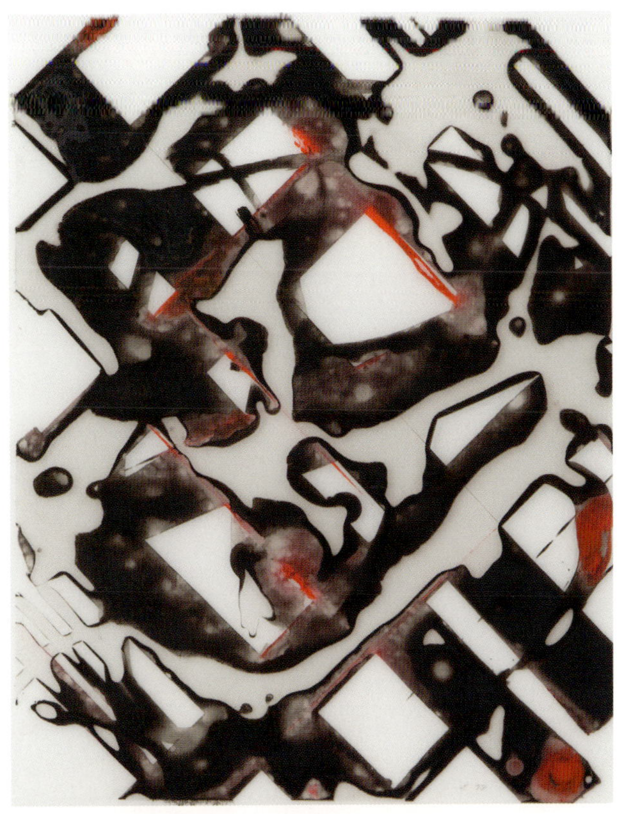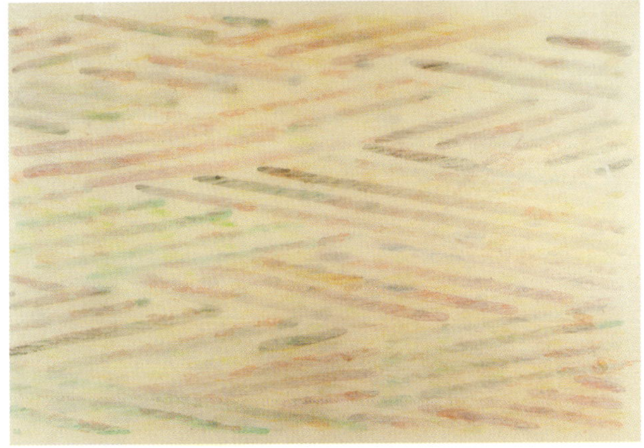

Ed Moses | Lar-e-et #4 | 1998 | Untitled | 1973

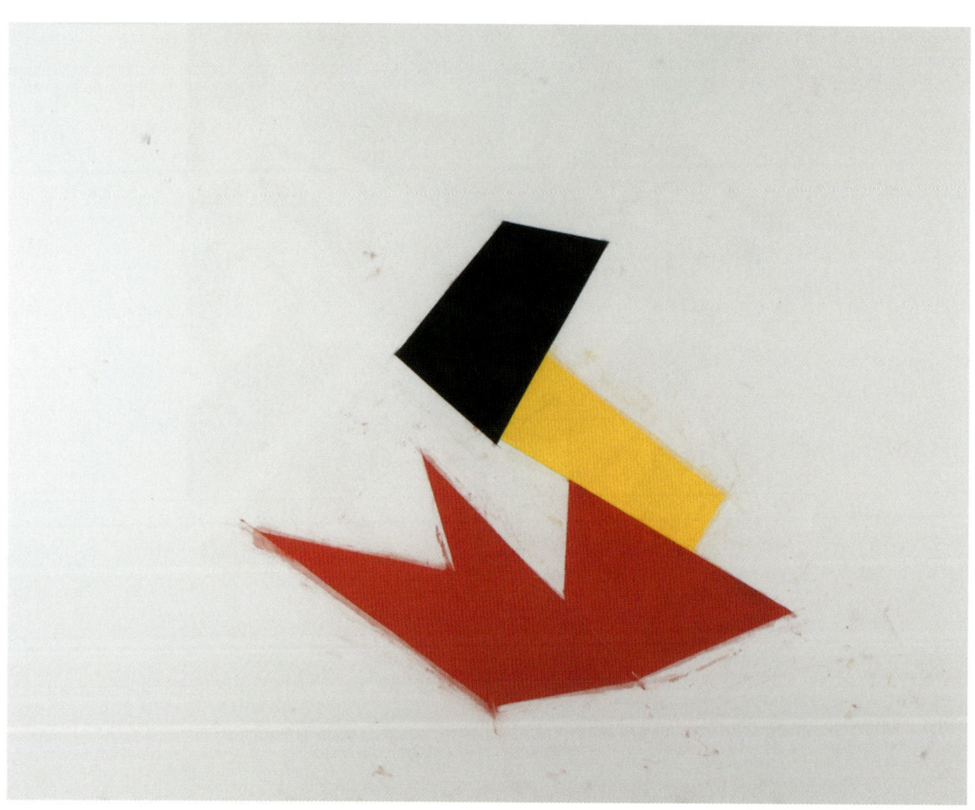

Joel Shapiro | Sketch for Boat, Bird, Mother and Child | 2008

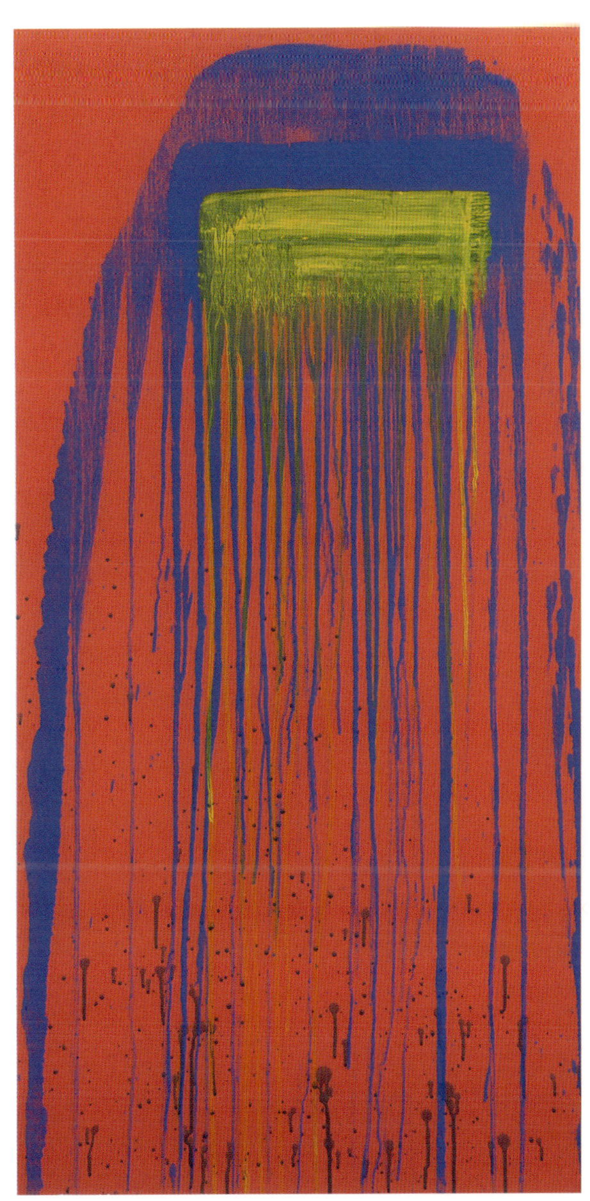

Pat Steir | Waterfall #23 | 2003

CHECKLIST

Peter Alexander | *Ylang Ylang* | 2004 | acrylic on paper | 16" x 19"

Charles Arnoldi | *Untitled* | 1998 | acrylic on canvas | 14" x 11"

Charles Arnoldi | *Untitled* | 1999 | gouache on collaged paper | 28" x 21"

Charles Arnoldi | *Untitled* | 2005 | acrylic on aluminum | 8" x 7 1/4"

Charles Arnoldi | *Volatile* | 2005 | acrylic on canvas | 24" x 97"

Walter Darby Bannard | *Blue March* | 1975 | acrylic resins on canvas | 51" x 41 1/2"

Michael Beck | *Naval Maneuvers* | 2006 | oil on canvas | 14 1/2" x 14"

Fletcher Benton | *Table 5* | 1989 | welded steel | 36 1/2" x 13" x 13 1/2"

Sonja Blomdahl | *Blomma Vase* | 2004 | hand blown glass | 13 3/8" x 8 7/8" diameter | created at Museum of Glass, Tacoma

William Brice | *Untitled* | 2007 | oil on canvas | 48" x 36"

Squeak Carnwath | *Untitled* | 1991 | monoprint on paper | 31 1/2" x 31 1/4"

Dale Chihuly | *Glass Painting* | 2001 | acrylic on paper, signed in glass | 41" x 29"

Dale Chihuly | *Red Blanket Cylinder* | 2000 | hand blown glass | 7 1/4" x 8 3/4" x 6 3/8"

Christo and Jeanne-Claude | *Wrapped Bottle and Cans (Project)* | 1958-2004 | lithograph on paper, 22/200 | 15" x 13 5/8"

Ronald Davis | *Three Squares (Flatland Series)* | 1980 | watercolor on Arches 300 paper | 60" x 40"

Mark di Suvero | *Nukle* | 2008 | titanium | 9" x 9" x 8"

Richard Diebenkorn | *Blue with Red* | 1987 | color wood block print on paper, 167/200 | 33 1/2" x 23"

Richard Diebenkorn | *Untitled #4* | 1965 | drypoint and etching on paper, artist's proof | 14 1/2" x 18 1/2"

Guy Dill | *Untitled Wall Sculpture* | circa 1988 | welded, painted steel | 29" x 22" x 32"

Laddie John Dill | *Untitled* | 1982 | cement, polymer resin, and glass on wood | 16" x 23 1/2"

Laddie John Dill | *Untitled* | 1983 | monoprint on paper | 27" x 63 1/4"

Jim Dine | *Hammer with Watercolors* | 1982 | lithograph with hand painted watercolor on paper, 24/46 | 44" x 61"

Maynard Dixon | *Mountain Wall – Lone Pine* | 1929 | oil on board | 9 1/8" x 13"

Maynard Dixon | *Skies of New Mexico #18* | 1931 | oil on board | 9 3/8" x 13 1/8"

Carlos Estrada-Vega | *Three Size Composition #5* | 2000 | oleopasto, wax and pigments on wood | 12" x 12"

Claire Falkenstein | *Untitled* | 1959 | fused colored glass fragments and metal rods | 5" x 8" x 5"

Claire Falkenstein | *Untitled* | circa 1960s-1970s | fused bottle glass and metal rods, sardine can with key, metal grate | 3" x 8" x 6"

Eric Fischl | *Study for Painting* | 1995 | watercolor on paper | 14 1/2" x 12 1/2"

Caio Fonseca | *Little Fifth* | 1999 | color softground and spit bite aquatint etching on paper, 16/50 | 17 7/8" x 21 1/4"

Sam Francis | *Handmade for Garner* | late 1970s | monotype with hand painting on paper | 34" x 34"

Sam Francis | *Untitled* | 1989 | acrylic on paper | 12 1/2" x 15"

Helen Frankenthaler | *A Page From A Book I* | 1997 | 24-color etching, aquatint, mezzotint, and pochoir on paper, 22/60 | 10 1/8" x 24 3/4"

Helen Frankenthaler | *A Page From A Book III* | 1997 | 14-color etching, aquatint, mezzotint, and pochoir on paper, 18/60 | 10 1/8" x 24 3/4"

Joe Goode | *Fire and Ice* | 2006 | mixed media on photographs | 32" x 48"

Robert Graham | *Elisa* | 1996 | bronze, 2/6 | 4" x 7" x 4 1/2"

Robert Graham | *Fragment Head* | 1994-1995 | bronze sculpture in two parts | 4" x 3" x 3 1/2"

Frederick Hammersley | *Ahead of time* | 1987 | oil on three-inch plywood | 8 1/2" x 7 3/4"

Otto and Vivika Heino | *Glaze Fired Bowl* | 1995 | stoneware with matte white glaze and Barnard slip decoration, thrown and decorated by Otto Heino | 2 1/2" x 13" diameter

David Hockney | *Big Celiaprint #1* | 1981 | lithograph on paper, 36/100 | 47" x 56"

Bryan Hunt | *Open Cross #2* | 1996 | bronze with limestone base, edition of 5 | 33" x 17" x 8 1/2"

Bryan Hunt | *Untitled* | 1996 | mixed media on Arches paper | 30 1/4" x 22 1/2"

Jasper Johns | *0 [Zero]* | 1975 | aquatint etching on paper, 74/100 | 8 3/8 " x 6"

Jun Kaneko | *Chunk #91-8-1* | 1991 | glazed ceramic | 7 1/2" x 10 3/8" x 12 3/8"

Jun Kaneko | *Dango #09-04-13* | 2009 | glazed ceramic | 23 1/2" x 21 1/4" x 11 1/2"

Jun Kaneko | *Hawaiian* | 1997 | sumi ink, oil stick on Korean rice paper | 37 1/2" x 26"

Alex Katz | *Vincent* | 1993 | color aquatint etching on paper, 9/30 | 37" x 23 3/4"

Ellsworth Kelly | *18 Colors (Cincinnati)* | 1979-1982 | 18-color lithograph on Arches Cover paper, 21/57 | 16" x 90 1/2"

Ellsworth Kelly | *Blue* | 2001 | color lithograph on Rives BFK paper | 29/45 | 37" x 29"

Jonathan Lasker | *Pictorial Regularity* | 2000 | oil on canvas board | 12" x 16"

Alfred Leslie | *Untitled* | 1953-54 | oil and mixed media collage on canvas | 7 3/4" x 7 3/4"

Sol LeWitt | *Bands (Not Straight) in Four Directions – Red* | 1999 | oil-base woodcut print on Zangestu paper, 27/75 | 14 1/4" x 35"

James Lovera | *Green Lava Bowl* | circa 2005 | volcanic glazed earthenware | 3 1/2" x 6 1/2" diameter

James Lovera | *Red Bowl* | 2005 | glazed porcelain | 2 1/2" x 7 1/2" diameter

Kim MacConnel | *Woman with Mirror, Gouache #5* | 2007 | gouache on paper | 6" x 6"

Tony Marsh | *Bowl (Radiance and Abundance Series)* | 2007 | ceramic with engobe | 7 1/2" x 19 1/2" x 15 1/2"

John Mason | *Square Hex, Charcoal with Tracers* | 2004 | ceramic | 12 1/2" x 14" x 10"

Joseph Patrick McMeekin | *The Brook* | 1901 | oil on canvas | 12" x 18 1/2"

Daniel Mendel-Black | *Shifter III* | 2001 | acrylic on plywood | 18 1/8" x 15"

Brad Miller | *Bowl* | 1997 | glazed earthenware | 2 1/2" x 12" diameter

Brad Miller | *Untitled* | 2001 | mixed media on paper | 20" x 14 3/4"

Peter Millett | *Blue Rhumba* | 2002 | acrylic on paper collage | 25" x 18"

Peter Millett | *Log* | 1998 | steel | 24" x 9" x 9"

Peter Millett | *Octo* | 2005 | 12-gauge steel | 48" x 48" x 12"

Ed Moses | *Lar-e-et #4* | 1998 | acrylic on mylar | 28" x 23"

Ed Moses | *Untitled* | 1973 | acrylic on laminated tissue paper | 36" x 55"

Robert Motherwell | *Alberti Elegy* | 1982 | lithograph on tan handmade Okawara paper, artist's proof XIII/XX | 14" x 15"

Robert Motherwell | *Beau Geste I* | 1989 | lithograph on paper, H.C. | 22" x 15"

Gertrud and Otto Natzler | *Bowl* | 1977 | reduction fired earthenware with Blue Nocturne glaze | 4" x 6 1/2" diameter

Raymond Saunders | *Remembering and Then Forgetting* | 2001 | mixed media with collage on board | 48" x 48"

Raymond Saunders | *Untitled* | 1995 | mixed media on wood | 21 1/4" x 21 1/4" x 2 1/4"

Italo Scanga | *Head 78* | 1986 | wood and oil paint | 15" x 10" x 7 1/2"

Italo Scanga | *Vase* | 1987 | hand blown glass and paint | 16" x 7 1/2" diameter

John Seery | *Lenny* | 1973 | acrylic on canvas | 41 1/2" x 48"

Richard Serra | *Circuit* | 1972 | three-color lithograph on Angoumois handmade paper, 14/50 | 29" x 42"

Richard Serra | *The Line of the Curve* | 2004 | 6-panel one-color etching on Somerset Satin white paper, 21/35 | 22" x 22" each sheet

Richard Serra | *Venice Notebook 2001, #1* | 2002 | etching on Fabriano Tiepolo paper, 40/60 | 16" x 18"

Joel Shapiro | *Sketch for Boat, Bird, Mother and Child* | 2008 | pastel on paper | 29 7/8" x 39 5/16"

Peter Shire | *Nuovo Bel Air Model* | 2007 | steel and enamel | 6" x 7" x 5 3/4"

Peter Shire | *Winged Victory Plates* | 2000 | glazed ceramic | set of two, 1 1/2" x 14 1/4" diameter each

Sara Sosnowy | *Small Circle Series 5* | 1996 | oil, dry pigment and string on canvas | 20" x 20"

Pat Steir | *Waterfall #23* | 2003 | screenprint with hand-painting and drawing | 56 1/2" x 32 1/4"

Wayne Thiebaud | *Bow Ties* | 1990 | lithograph, color trial proof | 22" x 20 7/8"

Bertil Vallien | *Intersection II* | 1998 | sandcasted glass | 5" x 7 1/2" x 6 1/2"

Peter Voulkos | *Tea Bowl* | 1990 | wood-fired stoneware | 4" x 7 1/2" x 6 1/2"

Peter Voulkos | *Tea Bowl* | 1999 | soda-fired stoneware | 6" x 8 1/2" x 7 1/2"

Marguerite Wildenhain | *Vessel* | circa 1985 | glazed ceramic | 6 3/4" x 4 3/4" diameter

William T. Wiley | *Canister Under the Banister* | 2002 | oil on canvas | 32" x 38"

William T. Wiley | *Punch Live* | 2004 | mixed media, papier mâché, cardboard box | 29" x 19" x 19"

Terry Winters | *Models for Synthetic Pictures* | 1994 | intaglio, open bite, spit bite and soft ground etching on Campi paper, 7/35 | 19 3/8" x 22 1/4"

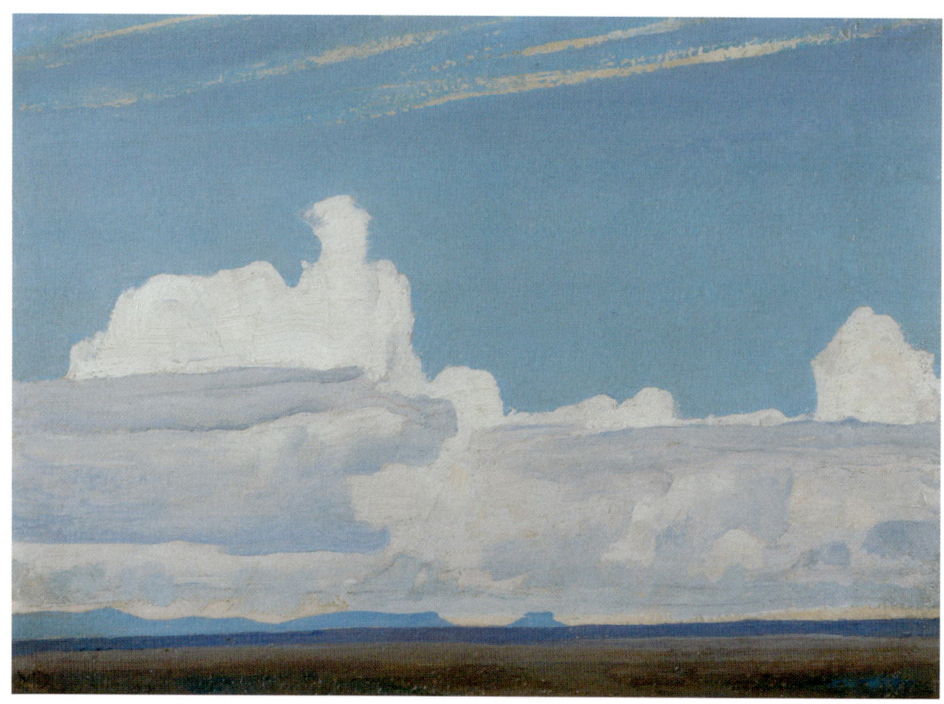

Maynard Dixon | Skies of New Mexico #18 | 1931

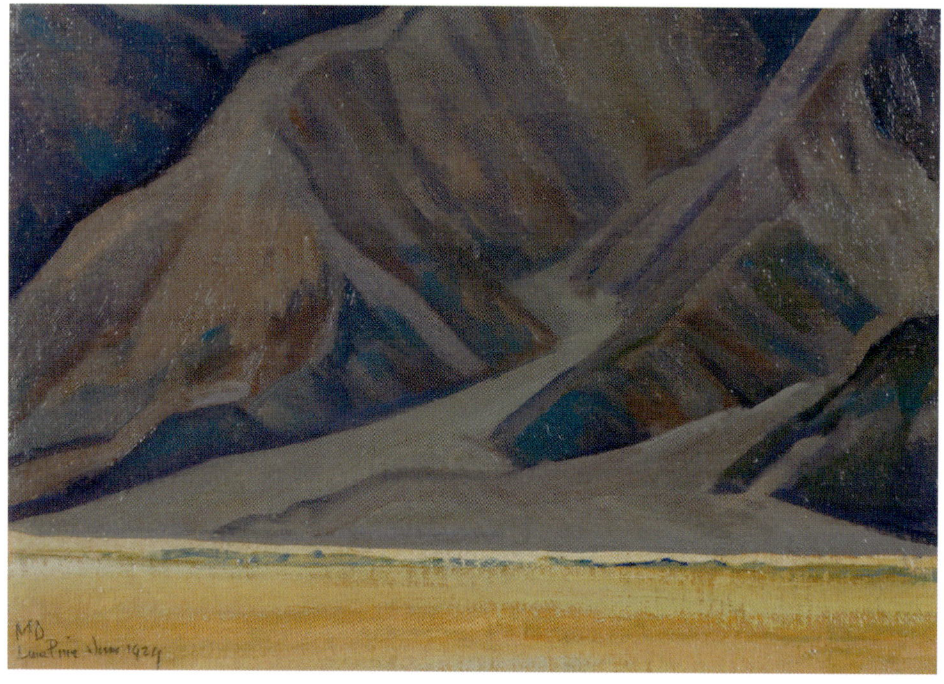

Maynard Dixon | Mountain Wall - Lone Pine | 1929

ACKNOWLEDGEMENTS

I would like to acknowledge Wilfred Davis Fletcher, whose belief in the Boise Art Museum's important work in this community led him to share his extraordinary collection with BAM. The works of art now belonging to Boise Art Museum's Permanent Collection will provide inspiration for exhibitions, programs, research, and teaching. The release of this publication is being made simultaneously with the announcement of a major financial gift from Wilfred Davis Fletcher, making possible the naming of a prominent gallery within the Museum in his honor. It is to Bill that I extend our profound appreciation for his generosity, sense of curiosity, sophisticated collecting vision, and friendship.

During the development of this project over the past several years, many people have played crucial roles in making this gift a reality. First, I owe a huge debt of gratitude to Jerry Young, Wilfred Davis Fletcher's assistant, for his commitment, including advocating for Bill's interests and those of the Museum. Without his encouragement and competent facilitation of everything from the management of Bill's collection database and organization of artwork for photographing, to communications between Idaho and California, this collaborative project would not have come to fruition. I appreciate his passion, devotion, and sense of humor. Cara Garcia is to be commended for her striking photography of the artworks under make-shift conditions. Her tenacity in capturing the best image for each work of art shines through. Chris Schnoor has encapsulated the essence of the collecting areas characterized by this gift of artworks to BAM with his insightful essays. Geoffrey Beard has designed the publication so that it showcases the group's endeavors in a stunning catalogue. I respect and thank each of these individuals for their expertise.

I further thank the artists whose works are included in the gifts documented in this book for their creativity and for responding to our inquiries. Gratitude is given to the artists' dealers and estate representatives for the information they provided.

I also wish to recognize the professional staff of the Boise Art Museum for the dedication and care given to this catalogue. In particular, Sandy Harthorn, Curator of Art, was responsible for leading the catalogue and its details. She undertook this immense project with her usual grace. Kathy Bettis, Registrar, coordinated the requirements for rights and reproductions, and the Library of Congress registration, as well as the editing. Their critical work was supported by the entire team of colleagues at the Boise Art Museum.

Finally, I would like to express my deep appreciation to the Board of Trustees of the Boise Art Museum for their ongoing support of BAM and its programs. Without their enthusiasm, the Museum would not be able to fulfill its educational mission.

Melanie Fales, Executive Director | CEO

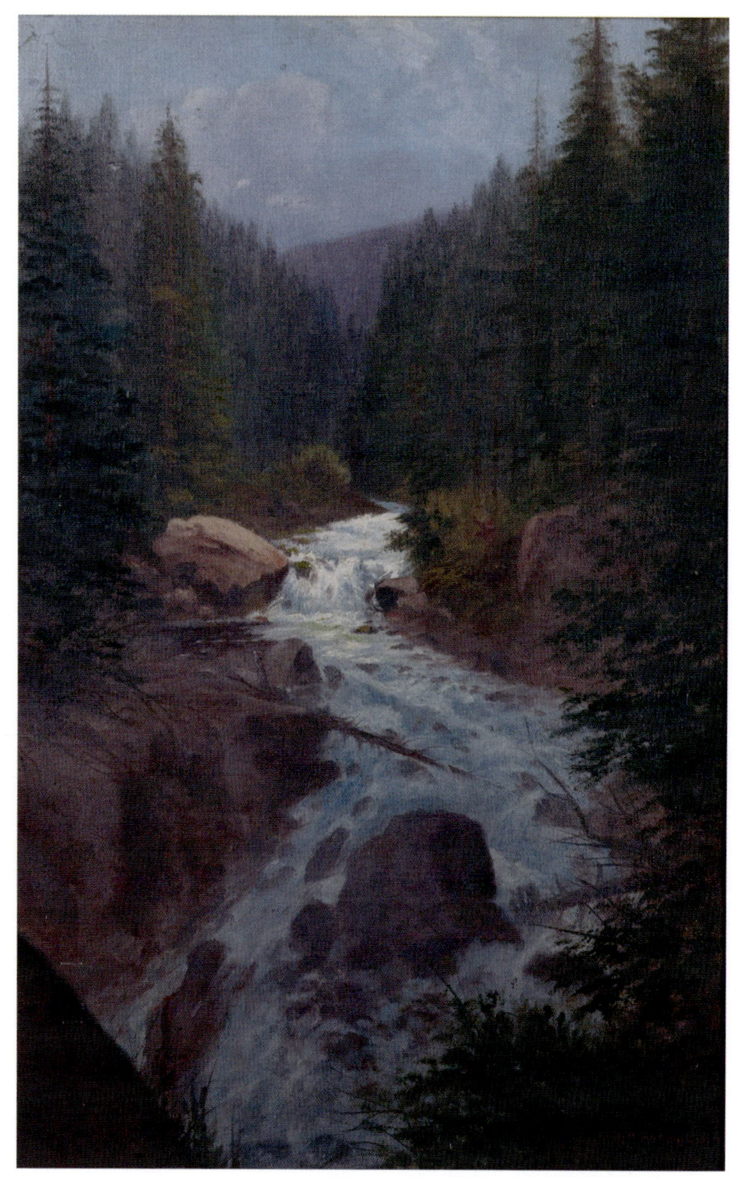

Joseph Patrick McMeekin | The Brook | 1901

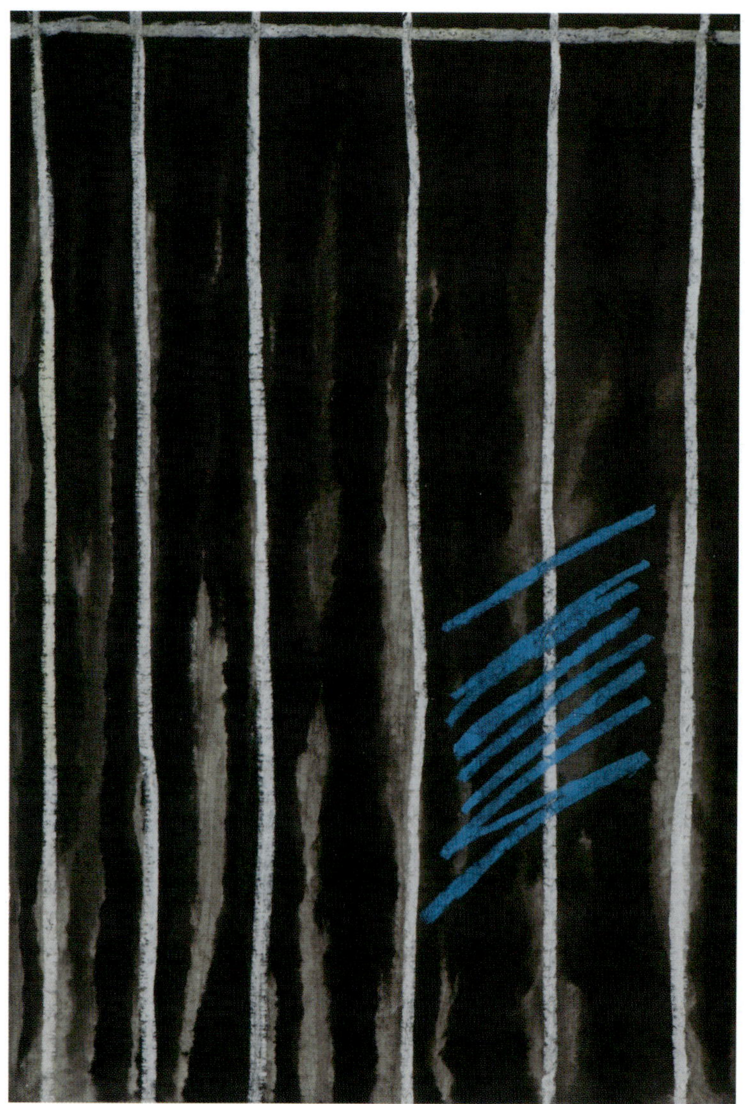

Jun Kaneko | Hawaiian | 1997

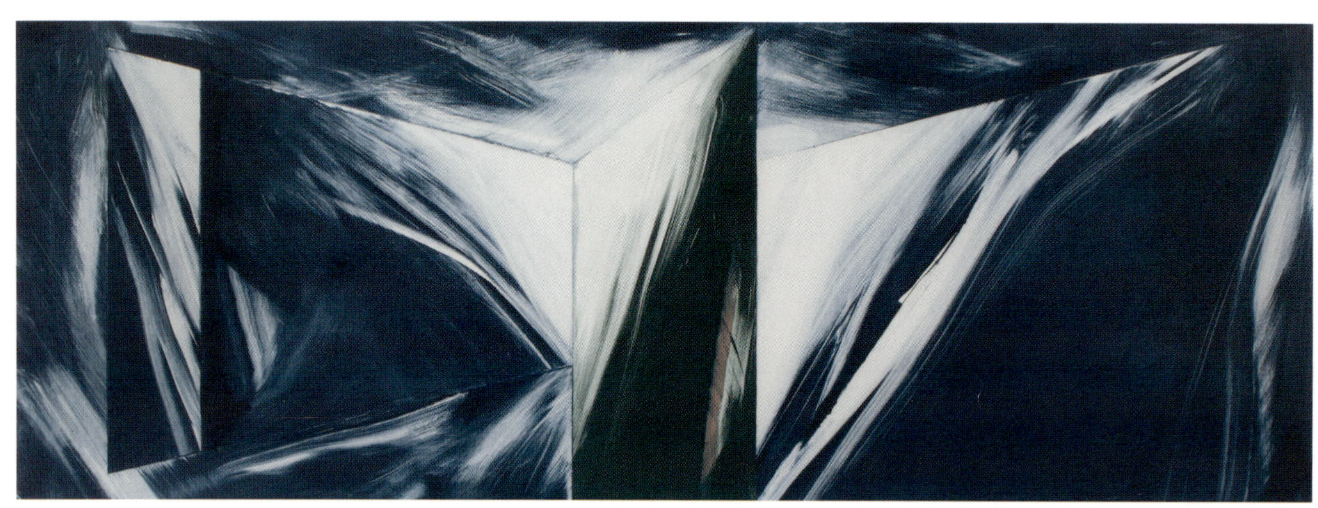

Laddie John Dill | Untitled | 1983

Printed in the United States of America

Essays | Christopher Schnoor
Photography | Cara Garcia | www.caragarcia.com
Design | Geoffrey Beard | geoff@jgc.me
Printing | Bridgetown Printing Company

Additional photography:
Dust jacket and page 6: Portrait of Wilfred Davis Fletcher © Menlo College | Page 2: Ellsworth Kelly, *Blue*, Photo courtesy the artist and Marquant Publications
Page 9: Portrait of Wilfred Davis Fletcher, Sun Valley, Courtesy of Wilfred Davis Fletcher
Pages 60 and 61: Ellsworth Kelly, *18 Colors (Cincinnati)*, Photo courtesy the artist and Marquant Publications
Page 75: Jun Kaneko, *Dango #09-04-13*, Photo courtesy Jun Kaneko Studio

Images are used by permission of the following artists:

Permission to reproduce images is granted by the artists and Artists Rights Society for the following images:
© 2012 Fletcher Benton / Artists Rights Society (ARS), New York | © 2012 Jim Dine / Artists Rights Society (ARS), New York
© Sam Francis Foundation, California / Artists Rights Society (ARS), New York
© 2012 Estate of Helen Frankenthaler / Artists Rights Society (ARS), New York, Courtesy Tyler Graphics Litd.
© 2012 Robert Graham Studio / Artists Rights Society (ARS), New York | © 2012 Bryan Hunt / Artists Rights Society (ARS), New York
© 2012 The LeWitt Estate / Artists Rights Society (ARS), New York | © 2012 Richard Serra / Artists Rights Society (ARS), New York
© 2012 Joel Shapiro / Artists Rights Society (ARS), New York

Permission to reproduce images is granted by the artists and VAGA, New York:
Art © Walter Darby Bannard/Licensed by VAGA, New York, NY | Art © Squeak Carnwath/Licensed by VAGA, New York, NY
Art © Jasper Johns and ULAE/Licensed by VAGA, New York, NY, Published by ULAE
Art © Alex Katz/Licensed by VAGA, New York, NY Art by Robert Motherwell © Dedalus Foundation, Inc. /Licensed by VAGA, New York, NY
Art © Wayne Thiebaud/Licensed by VAGA, New York, NY

© Peter Alexander | © Charles Arnoldi | © Michael Beck, Courtesy of Paul Thiebaud Gallery and Lora Schlesinger Gallery | © Sonja Blomdahl
Art by William Brice © Shirley Brice | © Chihuly Studio | © Christo 2004 | © Ronald Davis | © Mark di Suvero | © The Richard Diebenkorn Foundation | © Guy Dill
© Laddie John Dill | Art by Maynard Dixon | © John E. Dixon | © Carlos Estrada-Vega | Art by Claire Falkenstein © The Falkenstein Foundation | © Caio Fonseca Studio
© Joe Goode Studio | © Frederick Hammersley Foundation | Art by Otto and Vivika Heino © Helen Heino | © David Hockney / Gemini G.E.L.
© Ellsworth Kelly and Gemini G.E.L., Los Angeles, EK AX.193 | © Ellsworth Kelly and Gemini G.E.L., LLC, Los Angeles, EK AX.301 | © Jun Kaneko
© Jonathan Lasker, Courtesy Cheim & Read, New York | © Alfred Leslie | © James Lovera, Courtesy of Chris Winfield Gallery | © Kim MacConnel | © Tony Marsh
© Daniel Mendel-Black | © Brad Miller | © Peter Millett | © Ed Moses | Art by Gertrud and Otto Natzler © Gail Reynolds Natzler, Trustee, The Natzler Trust
© Raymond Saunders | Art by Italo Scanga © Katherine Scanga, Joseph Scanga, Italo Scanga Foundation | © John Seery | © Peter Shire | © Sara Sosnowy
© Pat Steir, Courtesy Cheim & Read, New York | © Bertil Vallien | Art by Peter Voulkos © Voulkos Family Trust | © Estate of Marguerite Wildenhain
© William T. Wiley | © Terry Winters, Courtesy Matthew Marks Gallery

Cover image: Charles Arnoldi | *Volatile* | 2005 | acrylic on canvas | 24" x 97" | Boise Art Museum Collection, Gift of Wilfred Davis Fletcher, 2012

Front section details:
Page 11 | Painting | William T. Wiley | *Canister Under the Banister* | 2002 | oil on canvas | 32" x 38" | *detail*
Page 31 | Sculpture | Fletcher Benton | *Table 5* | 1989 | welded steel | 36 1/2" x 13" x 13 1/2" | *detail*
Page 47 | Prints | Caio Fonseca | *Little Fifth* | 1999 | color softground and spit bite aquatint etching on paper, 16/50 | 17 7/8" x 21 1/4" | *detail*
Page 71 | Ceramics | Brad Miller | *Bowl* | 1997 | glazed earthenware | 2 1/2" x 12" diameter | *detail*
Page 85 | Glass | Italo Scanga | *Vase* | 1987 | hand blown glass and paint | 16" x 7 1/2" diameter | *detail*
Page 93 | Works on paper | Bryan Hunt | *Untitled* | 1996 | mixed media on Arches paper | 30 1/4" x 22 1/2" | *detail*

ISBN-10: 0964832615
ISBN-13: 978-0-9648326-1-9

Note on dimensions: All dimensions are for image size and are given in inches as height by width by depth, or height by diameter.

Boise Art Museum is a 501(c)(3) non-profit, educational, and charitable organization. The Museum is nationally accredited by the American Alliance of Museums.
Support is provided by BAM members, contributions and grants from individuals, corporations and foundations, as well as grant funding from the Idaho Commission on the Arts and the National Endowment for the Arts.

Library of Congress Cataloging-in-Publication Data

Boise Art Museum.
 In the abstract : Wilfred Davis Fletcher collection : paintings, sculpture, prints, ceramics, glass, works on paper / essays by Christopher Schnoor ; foreword by Melanie Fales ; introduction by Sandy Harthorn.
     pages cm
 Companion publication to American Art: Wilfred Davis Fletcher Collection, published by the Boise Art Museum in 2003.
 Includes bibliographical references and index.
 ISBN 978-0-9648326-1-9 (alk. paper)
 1. Art, American--20th century--Catalogs. 2. Art, American--21st century--Catalogs. 3. Fletcher, Wilfred Davis, 1922--Art collections--Catalogs. 4. Art--Private collections--Idaho--Boise--Catalogs. 5. Boise Art Museum--Catalogs. I. Schnoor, Christopher, 1949- II. Title.
 N6512.B56 2012
 709.73'07479628--dc22
                          2012040010